LAWFUL PURSUIT:
Careers in Public Interest Law

Ronald W. Fox

Edited by William D. Henslee
and Sara Vlajcic

**American Bar Association
Law Student Division
750 North Lake Shore Drive
Chicago, IL 60611**

Lawful Pursuit: Careers in Public Interest Law

ISBN: 1-57073-178-0

American Bar Association
750 North Lake Shore Drive
Chicago, Illinois 60611
(312) 988-5000

1 2 3 4 5 6 7 99 98 97 96 95

Contents

Preface

The American Bar Association's Career Series is designed to give students and beginning lawyers practical information on choosing and following career paths in the practice of law. Books in the series offer realistic, first-hand accounts of practicing law in specific substantive areas and guidance on setting and reaching career goals.

The Career Series evolved during the ABA's 1982 Annual Meeting as a joint project of the Section of Economics of Law Practice (now the Law Practice Management Section), the Law Student Division, and the Standing Committee on Professional Utilization and Career Development. Working together, these three entities formed the Career Series Steering Committee which is now the ABA's official clearinghouse for career-oriented publications. The members of this committee are lawyers, law students, and administrators who understand the need for educated career choices. They have geared the Career Series toward meeting the needs of students and lawyers contemplating career decisions.

Since 1982, many committee members have worked to produce this series of books, and we would like to thank some of them. Gary Munneke, Theodore Orenstein, Monica Bay, Thomas Wynn, Lynn Strudler, Carol Kanarek, Ellen Wayne, Peggy Podell, and Percy Luney have all been instrumental in establishing, developing, and maintaining the Career Series. In addition, the committee has relied on Sherry Gouwens and other ABA staff members.

Our committee's goal is to help lawyers secure satisfying jobs in their chosen areas of practice. To this end, the Career Series Steering Committee presents this publication to complement the Career Series.

William D. Henslee
Chairman
American Bar Association
Career Series Steering Committee

Acknowledgements

It took me some time to recognize that my resistance to preparing the acknowledgement was due to its importance. The opportunity to openly express your appreciation to those who have been the sources of your motivation, strength, inspiration, and knowledge is one of the most positive aspects of the entire endeavor.

I had no idea when I met John Barmack and he asked me to represent an association of public housing tenants that it marked the beginning of not only what continues to be a valued friendship, but also a twenty five year exploration of the delivery of legal services to the public. Paul Garrity taught many of us how to make things happen, guiding and supporting my first efforts to develop a program to connect lawyers to those with "personal plight" legal issues. For twenty years I have had the good fortune to work with Dan Burnstein, a lawyer and an educator, creating referral programs, legal clinics and a training institute founded on his quietly expressed vision of a just society. I also deeply appreciate his personal support and professional advice over the years.

Ellen Wayne, a true professional with integrity, knowledge, and experience, introduced me to the world of law school career planning. She was instrumental at the beginning of this project when she recommended me to the ABA Law Student Division publication committee as the author of this book. Her invaluable suggestions, comments, and support at the page proof stage helped complete the project.

The incentive to develop an approach to career planning for law students came because of the need to prepare workshop presentations for conferences I was invited to by Michael Caudell-Feagan.

Patricia Gimbel Epstein provided invaluable assistance for the first draft of the book. She contributed much of substance, developed forms, edited, and often got me past bouts of "writer's block." William Henslee provided continual support and encouragement as well as valuable comments on the first draft. Before receiving Bill's comments, however, I read: Gary Munneke's book, *From Law Student to Lawyer,* and the MacCrate Report. I learned so much from them that I found it necessary to substantially rewrite the book.

If it had not been for Sara Vlajcic, however, I would still be sitting at the computer. She added much clarity and greater coherence to my second draft as well as incorporating the responses I received from the lawyers quoted in the book. All this without in any way altering the sense or meaning of what I was attempting to convey.

Other valued friends and guides include Jeff Petrucelly, Burt Nadler, Claude Lancome, Richard Bourne, Dana Bullwinkel, and Mark Byers.

Thank you also to Lesley and Steve for your tolerance of your parents' ofttimes nontraditional views and career paths and to Chuck for the interest you have shown in this project. We know we are fortunate to have such caring and responsible children.

Most difficult is the attempt to compose a few phrases to thank my best friend of 40 years and wife of 33 years for all she has done for me and what she has meant to me. Suffice it to say that her unwavering sense of what is appropriate, fair, and just gave me the guidance, support, and strength to make choices over the years that have been uniquely rewarding and satisfying. For that alone I want to express my gratitude and my love.

Ronald W. Fox
February, 1995

Foreword

In 1947 at the age of eight I decided to be a lawyer and sent for a law school catalogue. During the next 7,300 days, I graduated elementary school, junior high, high school, college, and Harvard Law School.

While in law school, I attached no significance to the fact that I was perpetually miserable every day of the academic year, that I disliked and feared each class, and that I dreaded every assignment. In the summer between my first and second years, I cleaned dormitory rooms and when classes resumed in the fall I longed to be back scrubbing toilets. This should have been a big clue that the law might not be the field for me, but I ignored it and continued my legal studies. I found relief only in the post-dinner Scrabble game with my wife Joan.

After serving three delightful years in the U.S. Army Judge Advocate General's Corps in Albuquerque, I began my "real" life as an associate at a medium-sized Boston law firm in 1967. Twenty years after sending away for that law school catalogue, I found myself among competent, dedicated lawyers, who took depositions, filed claims, and occasionally went to court. It struck me like a thunderbolt, "My God, this is what lawyers really do." I hated it.

At the age of 28, I found myself really contemplating what it would mean to be a lawyer for the next forty years or so and dreading it. What should I do?

Being a child of the 50's, I was not sophisticated enough to know how to have a nervous breakdown. Instead, I became nearly clinically depressed and said, "No one can help me because my problem is just that I hate my job. Change the job and I'll be OK."

I believed, however, that in leaving this "upward" path, I would be taking a permanent detour for which I was sure I would have to endure the scorn and ridicule of my peers and family. Pressing on, I pored through an undergraduate placement directory and decided that I was not fit for anything else. Law school had taught me that I was already on the right track to become a "success." My clearest recollection, however, is of looking at one partner and saying to myself, "There's no way that's going to be me in fifteen years. In fact, there's no way that's going to be me next year."

I automatically rejected an offer with the new Greater Boston Legal Services program. Without really looking into the position, I imagined the work to be limited to sending letters to Sears about a defective dishwasher.

Instead, I accepted an offer to work for a life insurance company even though I had heard in law school that in-house counsel is for "losers." The grapevine also said that there is no real work to do there. That sounded good to me. I would have the time to decide what I wanted to do next. My friends and family did not reject me.

One year later, I felt the need to seek a more professionally rewarding experience and thought that a small firm experience in a small city might be worth a try. Despite the feeling I was sinking to a new low, I returned to my hometown of Lynn, Massachusetts, and worked for a wonderful person who tolerated my decision to represent public housing tenants for no fee. I began to rethink my low opinion about the practice of law outside the setting of the medium or large firms.

My experiences led to starting a law firm with another attorney who wanted to represent individuals and community groups. I began to concentrate on family law, including divorce mediation as an alternative to the litigation approach. My work took on new meaning as I offered clients a more effective and appropriate means of resolving intrafamily disputes.

At the same time, I became aware of how few lawyers were available to represent people with serious and critical legal concerns. I began trying to find ways that my firm and other lawyers could earn a living helping people instead of representing commercial institutions. I devoted substantial time to establishing programs to increase the quality and quantity of legal services delivered to the public: helping to restructure Neighborhood Legal Services of Lynn; creating the Housing Court Referral Project for the Massachusetts Bar Association Legal Services to the Poor Committee; organizing the Association of Neighborhood Law Clinics; co-directing the Lawyer Referral Service of the Massachusetts Chapter of the National Lawyers Guild which created a lead paint panel and a group legal services program; and serving as president of the Massachusetts Council for Family Mediation.

For years I had been aware that my skills and interests were not compatible with "traditional" law practice which relied heavily on courts and the adversary system. When I had the opportunity to start an organization to provide professional development programs for lawyers, I took it and dissolved my law firm.

This led to an offer to advise law students at Harvard Law School on how to pursue a career in public interest law. What better way to increase the quantity and quality of services delivered to the public than to encourage law students to follow this path after graduation? I quickly discovered, however, that law schools, consciously or unconsciously, steer students away from public interest careers. Without active encouragement or programs in this field, law schools tend to perpetuate the commonly held myths about public interest legal careers.

At Harvard, I directed efforts to remove barriers that kept law students from entering public service: providing individual guidance and developing workshops; establishing staff committees; putting together manuals and directories; coordinating grant programs; and co-founding the Public Interest Task Force of the National Association for Law Placement.

After I was there five years, a new dean arrived and informed me a month later that he was eliminating my position. At the age of 50, I had the "opportunity" to redirect my career path.

I recognized that the counseling I had been doing at Harvard was the most satisfying work I had ever done as a lawyer. To continue this work, I started the Public Interest Law Career Planning Center. As its executive director, I counsel lawyers and law students seeking public interest positions, both individually and in workshops. I also consult with law schools and bar associations developing programs to support those who want to use their training to serve the legal needs of the public.

Looking back over the last 26 years, what strikes me is that to a great extent I had to overcome the motivation that drove me from age 8 to 28 following the traditional career path of a lawyer. I had steered away from public interest law because I bought into the myth that in order to be successful, I had to do exactly what other people and large institutions wanted me to do; i.e., serve *their* best interests.

Since 1970, however, and perhaps ironic to say in a book on public interest, my work in the field of public interest has been guided by self-interest, a commitment to doing what I felt was best for me and my family. I reject the notion that the guiding impulse was a sense of altruism. I did it because it was important to me, it was deeply satisfying, and I felt proud of my work—a selfish foundation for choosing a career path. I encourage you to do the same!

1
Introduction

For the last ten years, I have listened to anguished practicing lawyers wanting to leave their jobs.

Some say their work is boring, unchallenging, or meaningless. Former editors of law reviews tell us they can't even send out a cover letter without a partner making substantial changes.

Others complain of work that conflicts with their strongest held values and believe they are always defending the "wrong" side; i.e., the manufacturer of the children's clothing that caught fire, the illegal dumper of poisonous waste, the employer who discriminates against women. Female attorneys and minority lawyers complain about unfair treatment, and yet hesitate to use their legal training to do anything about it.

I listen to lawyers who say they hate to go to work each day. They feel underused, misused, and abused. They believe they have lost control over the direction of their careers and their lives. Disillusioned and dissatisfied, they only want to do "something that matters."

This feeling of dissatisfaction is quite prevalent among lawyers, not just those who come to us for career guidance. A recent ABA Young Lawyer's Division survey found that 66% of all lawyers would change jobs within two years if they had a "reasonable alternative option." (*The State of the Legal Profession—Report #1—A Discussion of the Extent, Causes and Impact of Lawyers' Career Dissatisfaction 1990 v. 1984*, 1990.) A California survey found that 70% of the lawyers responding said that if they had the opportunity to start a new career they would take it and 73% said they would not suggest law as a career to their children. (March 1992, *California Lawyer.*)

From High Hopes to No Hope

Oddly enough, most of these same lawyers entered law school with high hopes and expectations. In my work advising students at Harvard Law School in the 1980s, my records, conversations, and surveys confirmed that at least 40% of each class entered law school planning to work for social justice, the social good, or simply to help people who need their help and "do something that matters." Discussions with career advisers at other law schools confirm that the percentage of students who are drawn to public interest law at their schools is just as high. Indeed, many take positive steps in that direction while still in law school.

And yet, by the time they are ready to graduate, the vast majority of law students are intent on finding a position which conforms to someone else's definition of success. Not surprisingly, each year, upon graduation, over 90% of the class at many law schools took positions brutally in conflict with their visions.

An analysis of one class revealed that of 550 graduates, twelve entered government, nine took legal services positions and eight took other traditional public interest positions. Not one of these new graduates was likely in the next few years to represent a low-income tenant, a student, an employee, a woman seeking a divorce, or any other one of the millions of non-indigent members of society.

The extensive work of Professor David Chambers of the University of Michigan Law School documents the substantial decrease over the last two decades in the percentage of those taking positions serving individuals with urgent personal plight problems upon graduation, especially from the many schools which describe themselves as the "best" law schools.

So how do law students journey from wanting to work for social justice to being a dissatisfied practicing attorney? My belief is that the primary cause of rampant dissatisfaction of so many within the legal profession can be ascribed to the law schools which fail to teach students the values of 1) recognizing their professional and personal goals, 2) improving their skills, and 3) promoting justice in their work. Rather than encourage students to pursue a career in the public interest, law schools generally divert their students from following that type of career path.

Most of my time counseling students was devoted to attempting to provide facts and resources to counter the pressure and propaganda from the law school, peers, family, friends, and the media whose advice included simplistic, but seductive definitions of *success, prestige,* and *income.* I understood that pressure because I had accepted the same definitions while in school and after graduation when I accepted a position with a Boston law firm. It was only later that I realized that those definitions may work for others, but I felt something was missing.

The purpose of this book is to help law students and dissatisfied practicing attorneys explore the public interest law in search of ways to fill in that missing piece and make their professional life more complete. It may be in the public interest, but it is in your own interest, too, to make sure your professional life does not contain that gap which leaves so many lawyers feeling dissatisfied.

America's Underrepresented

Looking around, you'll find no shortage of people who need your legal skills and training. In urban areas, seven out of ten children have higher than normal levels of lead in their bloodstream. Many are retarded, many in danger of losing their kidneys. Who represents them?

And problems aren't limited to the big cities. In my hometown of Lynn, Massachusetts, where I practiced law for fifteen years, there were 1,291 reports of child abuse filed in a recent year. Fortunately, for some of the affected children there is a Lynn-based law firm, the Children's Law Project of Massachusetts, which can represent a few of these children. Who represents the rest of the children in Lynn and those in Salem, Fall River, or the other 349 cities and towns in Massachusetts? Who represents the children in Portland, Maine or Portland, Oregon?

Lloyd Cutler, until recently legal counsel to President Clinton and a senior partner in the Washington, D.C. firm of Wilmer, Cutler and Pickering, summed it up in 1980 with the following observation:

> The rich who pay our [lawyer] fees are less than 1% of our fellow citizens, but they get at least 95% of our time. The disadvantaged who we serve for nothing are perhaps 20–25% of our population and get at most 5% of our time. The remaining 75% cannot afford to consult us and get virtually none of our time.

If the recent *New York Times* report which stated that in the 1980s only one group saw their tax burden reduced—the wealthiest 1%—is accurate, then the legal profession may be able to take much of the credit for this. Even those who are eligible for low-cost or free legal assistance receive only a fraction of the help they need. The March 1988 issue of the *ABA Journal* noted one study which found that all the neighborhood legal services programs and all law firm pro bono efforts provide representation to the disadvantaged in only one of every fourteen of their legal problems. Other studies have estimated that anywhere from ninety to ninety-seven percent of the public cannot afford a lawyer for their basic legal needs. The net result is that the legal system serves well less than four million people and leaves out of the justice system about 246 million members of our society.

Derek Bok noted in 1982 that "The blunt inexcusable fact is that this nation, which prides itself on efficiency and justice, has developed a legal system that is the most expensive in the world, yet cannot manage to protect the rights of most of its citizens."

If we truly believe that the Constitution guarantees everyone access to the American legal system, it is indefensible that our society has allowed this situation to develop where over two hundred million men, women, and children with health, housing, employment, education, civil rights, and family legal issues are unable to obtain representation.

During the years I was involved in establishing legal referral programs and other delivery systems, there was never a problem finding areas of unmet legal needs whether it was tenants' rights, lead paint victims, abused spouses, immigration, or discrimination. There is no shortage of environmental causes worth fighting for, from saving trout streams to saving an entire species of animals. Inequities plague our justice system, but it remains your choice to simply throw up your hands in frustration or use your legal skills to improve the laws and the system.

Your legal education and advocacy skills offer you the opportunity to do important work for the underrepresented, whether it is individuals, groups, or issues that concern you. Maybe you entered law school knowing exactly who it is or what cause you want to serve. Perhaps you have only a vague idea of "doing something that matters."

But whether your image is clear or still needs fine tuning, you have a vision of what it means to practice law. Although along the way there will be those who may try to divert you from your vision, there are also many others working to provide support.

Recently, the Public Services Division of the American Bar Association sponsored a Town Meeting in Washington, DC. Participants in the program, co-sponsored by the Law Student Division of the ABA, included students, faculty and staff from all the law schools in the district and representatives of NALP and NAPIL. ABA President George E. Bushnell, Jr. gave the opening address, encouraging the group to discuss ways the ABA and the law school community can work together to overcome the obstacles faced by law students poised to serve the public's interests.

During the two hour session, which Anne Dunn, staff liaison of the ABA Public Services Division, coordinated and I facilitated, participants considered a number of barriers and proposed solutions to reduce their effect. Among the suggestions were the integration into the traditional curriculum of courses designed to teach legal skills, the values of the legal profession, the wide range of options and profession development (career decision making and career planning).

Because of the enthusiasm reflected by the participants and the interest they expressed in being involved in follow-up sessions, the ABA Public Services Division and the Law Student Division intend not only to continue to work with this group but to organize similar efforts in other cities. If there is one near you, get involved and be a participant.

If you want to use your skills pursuing legitimate claims of the underrepresented or if you want to better society by working for social and economic justice, I challenge you to find one reason why you can not do so. The underlying principle of this book is that you simply need to take control over all important decisions relating to your professional development, your work—what you are going to do, with whom, and for whom—and your life.

2
Three Career Settings for Serving the Public's Interests

With few having the power to pursue legitimate claims and right wrongs done to them, to seek remedies for illegal acts and tortious conduct committed against them, there is little danger that the definition we will craft of careers serving the public's interests will be too broad. This area of law includes attorneys who use their legal training to promote justice by representing individuals, groups, causes, or issues identified as traditionally under-represented or unrepresented. Through this representation, lawyers help to balance the scales of justice and move society a little closer to fulfilling its goal of providing equal access to the justice system.

We can initially divide careers serving the public's interests into three settings:

1. public law firms (which includes public interest litigation organizations, public defender programs, and legal services offices);
2. non-profit organizations; and
3. private law firms.

There are also many opportunities to serve the public's interests working for a government entity. See the ABA Career Series book *Now Hiring: Government Jobs for Lawyers*.

Public Law Firms

When most people think of public interest careers for lawyers, they probably envision the types of positions which fall in this category. Public law firms include public interest litigation organizations, public defender programs, and legal services offices.

Public Interest Litigation Organizations

There are only a few public interest litigation organizations in the country. While there are only about 3,300 lawyers in such positions, many have achieved some spectacular results and are held in high regard by the legal profession and society in general. Public interest litigators understand that test cases or class action suits filed by their organizations have the potential to affect entire groups of people and society, not just individual clients.

Such organizations usually limit their involvement to one or two areas of the law such as education, housing, employment, health, or civil rights. Some well-known examples include the NAACP Legal Defense Fund and the Mexican-American Legal Defense and Education Fund (MALDEF) which work in the area of civil rights, the American Civil Liberties Union (ACLU), which protects civil liberties, and the Natural Resources Defense Counsel (NRDC), Conservation Law Foundation, and the Sierra Club Legal Defense Fund, all of which seek to protect the environment.

There are organizations which serve members of a particular segment of society such as consumers (Public Citizen), gays and lesbians (Lambda Legal Defense and Educational Fund), women (NOW Legal Defense and Education Fund), ethnic groups or minorities (Native American Legal Defense Fund.)

The Children's Defense Fund protects society's youngest members in the areas of education, special needs, health and welfare, neglect, and delinquency prevention while the Legal Counsel for the Elderly serves senior citizens. There are public interest litigators who defend the rights of immigrants, tenants, welfare recipients, the physically and mentally disabled, and animals.

Attorneys who work for these organizations become involved in various aspects of complex civil litigation, frequently class action suits or test cases on significant issues affecting many individuals to protect their rights. Such cases are initiated to effect social change or reform some agency or institution. The work may include legal and factual research, writing, and other aspects of lawsuits at the trial or appellate level.

The size of the legal staff may range from one attorney to the 36 working for the Natural Resources Defense Council. Openings are infrequent and when they occur, they are usually widely advertised. Since these organizations have a high profile and good reputations, there may be anywhere from 300 to 1,000 applicants.

Many of the attorneys who work for public interest litigation organizations spend time being interviewed by the media themselves or counseling other staff people who may be interviewed or hold a news conference. These lawyers often find it necessary to respond to negative publicity or crisis situations involving their organization.

At these organizations and particularly where staff size is small, the attorneys perform a wider variety of tasks, as opposed to the monotony encountered by many starting out at a large private firm or corporation. The work of Susan Vivian Mangold at the Juvenile Law Center in Philadelphia illustrates this diversity. Her work involved a mixture of litigation, research, policy-development, and counseling individual children. The office was also involved in class action suits to address the needs of children in the dependency and delinquency systems and regarding health care services to indigent families.

"I had primary responsibility for one class action suit claiming a right to aftercare services for children in the delinquency system in Philadelphia," explains Mangold. "This suit involved fascinating questions as to the limits of judicial power and we worked with a team of academics to fine tune our arguments. The settlement process in this case also involved scholarly experts who helped us devise a model system of aftercare services."

As part of her responsibilities, Mangold led training for judges, lawyers, doctors, and social workers on the child protective services system. She co-edited two books, including a judicial deskbook and a manual titled *Child Abuse and the Law* used for training. Working with law student interns, she developed a series of fact sheets on a variety of topics regarding children and the law which were used to respond to frequent telephone requests for information.

"Each of us in the office had a different policy focus," Mangold explains. "I concentrated on health issues and drafted the state policy for HIV–involved children under state custody. I also worked with the Education Law Center to put together a statewide coalition to address the delivery of preventive health services to Medicaid eligible children."

Today, Mangold teaches at State University of New York (SUNY) at Buffalo, School of Law, a career move she made to have more private time with her husband and two young sons.

"At SUNY, I am using yet another strategy to address the needs of children in state care," she says. "I teach Child Advocacy and the

Law and Evidence and the Child Victim. Both give me an opportunity to collect the literature in this area of law and to teach students about the fascinating legal issues inherent in representing children."

In addition to classwork, Mangold is developing plans for a Child Advocacy Clinic, working with students to devise protocols for agencies which respond to domestic violence on how they can best serve the children involved. The work will be used as models by the state's Office for the Prevention of Domestic Violence.

"I have redefined my job description in an ongoing evolution that is partly influenced by my career goals and partly by my personal needs," she says. "It has always worked out fine and I really encourage law students to remain idealistic concerning their goals and options."

Mangold describes her active involvement with children even as a college student and law school student which helped prepare her for her present career.

> My career has followed a fairly linear path with a focus on using my skills to improve the lives of children. That has meant different things at different times, but in each chapter of my career to date, I have used my intellect, my interpersonal skills, and my creative energy to focus on different ways in which our society looks at children and responds to their needs.

In college, Mangold ran a Big Brother/Big Sister project and then began a summer program in Cambridge housing projects to work with children. After college, she was the first program director for an inner–city Girls Club which provided everything from meals to recreation and counseling.

In law school, she co-founded the Children's Rights Project and expanded the Legal Aid Bureau's caseload to include representation of children. She interned at the Children's Defense Fund and began working at the Juvenile Law Center upon graduation. Mangold points out that even though she has recently left practice for academics, her work enables her to continue her role as an advocate for children.

"The particular setting of my work, the tasks of that job, and the strategies used to perform it have never been as important to me as the substantive area of working on behalf of children's needs," she says.

Mangold's interpersonal skills allow her to work extensively with professionals from other disciplines, such as social workers, doctors, and mental health experts. Her ability to convey to these groups of people and her students how the law influences the lives of children is key to her work. Her skills as a negotiator have helped her succeed in policy development and litigation. Law students considering this avenue of work would do well to develop similar skills.

The caring aspect of her work is one shared by other lawyers who choose to be an advocate, whether they represent children, the elderly, the environment, or any other field of interest. It means having a clear set of goals, whether you are in a courtroom or a classroom, and keeping those goals in mind, whether you are at the beginning of your legal career or at mid-point—like Mangold—with a young family demanding much of your time.

"At the risk of being sappy, I want to convey that the substance of my work still gets to me and I still care deeply about the lives and issues involved," according to Mangold.

She recalls one day after successfully trying a very difficult case in Family Court, she was headed back to her office when she witnessed a poignant scene:

> I saw a social worker with two young boys walking back to the child welfare office. She was holding the hand of a toddler and he was hanging onto his older brother with his other hand. The toddler was crying and the older boy was dragging a garbage bag filled with their personal belongings in his free hand. That image of children being 'cared for by the state' has always stayed with me. I don't know the circumstances that had brought these two boys to be with the social worker. Much more violent and needy scenarios crossed my desk daily, but they never had the impact that that scene did. My own sons are now the approximate age of those boys, about 2 and 5, and just thinking of those two children dragging that bag along the sidewalk makes me cry.

It is true that this type of work can be emotionally challenging. Attorneys who choose it must accept the fact that they will not always win the battle, or like Mangold describes, even when they do win, they know there are many others who have no one to fight for them. It is easy to become depressed about what happens in the courtroom or through "the system."

Keep in mind, though, that while public interest litigators are occasionally disheartened by what goes on, their role as policy developers offers them a better chance than the average attorney to actually do something about it. If you care passionately about your field of interest and have a strong desire to work for change, working with a public interest litigation organization will enable you to do so.

Public Defender Programs

Public defender offices serve as court-appointed counsel for indigent defendants in criminal cases. The funding sources are federal, state, and local. Attorneys in these offices usually receive extensive experience doing factual investigation, interviewing clients and witnesses, researching legal issues and writing briefs, and presenting motions and trying cases before juries. Like those who work for public interest litigation organizations, they find the workload is varied and the level of responsibility is high.

Cases range from drunk driving cases to domestic violence, assault and battery, arson, white-collar crime, and murder.

Public defenders (PDs) spend time in person or on the phone with clients, witnesses, and other lawyers including assistant district attorneys. As part of their work, they visit crime scenes and investigate facts; do legal research; write briefs, motions and memos; prepare for court, present motions, and try cases with or without a jury.

The work is described by many PDs as far from routine, challenging, exciting, and rewarding. Miriam Conrad, who has worked as both a state public defender and currently as a federal defender, says her routine varies greatly.

"I could spend an entire day researching and writing an appeals brief, or visiting clients in jail," she explains. "If I am working on a trial, I spend at least half the day in court and the other half preparing witnesses, reviewing exhibits, or researching legal issues. When I'm not on trial, I make an average of two or three court appearances a week for preliminary examinations or bail hearings, motions or pretrial conferences."

In addition to court appearances, Conrad does "factual investigation, although most is handled by our paralegals and investigators." She meets regularly with prosecutors to negotiate pleas and spends a "substantial amount of time reviewing discovery, whether undercover tape recordings or documents relating to financial transactions."

Her experience as a state public defender was quite different, according to Conrad, and she spent much more time in court, generally six hours a day. Her caseload was about twice what it is now in federal court and so as a state defender she spent much more time negotiating pleas, meeting with clients, and investigating facts, and much less time doing research and writing.

"I feel that my need for intellectual stimulation is met by my work in federal court more than it was in state court," she reports.

"On the other hand, I have less opportunity now than I had in state court to hone my trial skills."

Her work as a defender enables her to fulfill personal and professional goals Conrad has set for herself.

> One of the goals which is satisfied by my work is having direct contact with clients who are people, rather than corporate entities. I derive great satisfaction from my relationships with my clients. I think that clients, especially in federal court, often feel overwhelmed by the power of the government that is prosecuting them and they greatly appreciate someone standing up for them and for their rights. I find this very gratifying at the same time that I wish that my efforts were more frequently successful.

Like many other defenders, Conrad describes her colleagues as supportive.

"In both the state and federal offices, I have enjoyed a non-hierarchical atmosphere, with supporting and collegial coworkers," she reports. "Both jobs have provided me with tremendous autonomy and with frequent opportunities to be creative."

Her work in the Federal Defender Office in Boston is significantly better compensated financially than the state defender position.

"Although obviously I did not become a public defender to get rich, I found the lack of financial reward and support at the state office demoralizing," Conrad says. "It's one thing to make less than classmates at big firms; it's another to go without cost of living increases, to scrounge for legal pads, and to be forced to work a week without pay in order to balance the office's budget."

While both jobs require long hours, the autonomy she has now allows her "to choose to a large extent when and how to put in a big chunk of time."

She describes her greatest concern as:

> the overwhelming odds against defendants in federal court—as a result of more careful screening of the cases chosen for prosecution, less favorable law, and a less sympathetic jury pool—will deprive me of a feeling of accomplishment. I don't mind if victories are few and far between, so long as they occur. It remains to be seen whether the lower success rate will lead to burnout. In state court, I worried about a different prospect: turning into a cog, cranking out pleas. At this point, I still feel a sense of accomplishment.

Key skills needed to succeed as a PD include legal analysis and reasoning, brief writing, advocacy, trial skills, legal research, counseling clients, factual investigation, negotiating, adversarial skills, and "street smarts," according to Conrad. She advises students considering this type of career to "use law school to try things on for size," especially through clinical programs.

My experience in a clinical program for prosecutors showed me that I wanted to practice criminal law, but as a defender rather than a prosecutor. Figure out what kind of work environment you like, how important autonomy is to you, whether you need to feel connected with your clients. The LIPP program made the financial drawbacks less troubling than they might have been otherwise—take advantage of it! Think about what your daily work life will be like. Even if you think you're interested in the substantive aspects of the work, you won't last long if you don't enjoy the daily activities that go with it.

Legal Services Offices

There are over 300 legal services programs in the country. Traditionally this name has been given to non-profit corporations which receive a significant portion of their funding from the Legal Services Corporation (LSC), a semi-autonomous federal corporation whose board of directors is appointed by the President.

Guidelines of the LSC limit eligibility for services to "indigents" and define this status. They also restrict the kinds of cases which may be taken by grantee agencies.

The LSC has established 17 back-up centers which act as support centers and clearinghouses for all Legal Services offices, each one having a specialty area. These include the National Health Law Center, the Center for Law and Education, and the National Consumer Law Center.

Most cases involve individual representation in housing; welfare, social security, and other government benefit cases; immigration; and family law (including spousal abuse) areas. The lawyer's caseload could involve eviction, unemployment compensation claims, school expulsions, foreclosures, loss of income, divorce, hearings on utility rates, refugee resettlement, juvenile court hearings, non-profit corporations, community economic development, and deportation hearings.

The attorneys usually have extensive client contact and gain invaluable experience, both in court and at administrative hearings arguing motions, preparing briefs, conducting depositions, negotiating, and presenting evidence and trying cases. The affirmative nature of the representation often leads to working with client groups on challenging complex civil cases with law reform implications in any one of the described areas.

Students in their first and second year often are able to find funding for summer internships with these offices. Unfortunately there are too few openings in Legal Services offices for full-time positions and because they are usually well advertised, hundreds of resumes are submitted for each position. Anyone interested should still apply but recognize that the likelihood of securing such a position is small unless he or she has early on begun to be involved in this area, through classes or clinics while still in law school.

Barbara Sard, managing attorney of the Consolidated Housing and Homelessness Unit of Greater Boston Legal Services (GBLS), describes her work as being varied. She supervises attorneys and paralegals on a full range of legal matters, from class action lawsuits to welfare department hearings concerning emergency shelter. She provides legal advice to the Massachusetts Coalition for the Homeless, works with housing and homeless advocates in other states on federal administrative and legislative issues, and devotes from 20 to 40 percent of her time on litigation or policy advocacy matters at the state or federal levels. She also handles a variety of miscellaneous management tasks, including fundraising, planning, and GBLS personnel matters.

Sard's position involves "conceptualizing and working to accomplish policy changes to make life better for a significant number of socially neglected people." She finds both an "intellectual and practical challenge of developing and implementing new legal strategies and leading others to accomplishing them." Among the positive factors of her work, she finds a diversity of people to work with who share common values and a mutually supportive environment while helping others grow. She enjoys her experiences with human and institutional reality versus what she describes as a "think tank" or public interest law firm isolation.

Her work is not without its negative aspects, however, including the fact that "job demands always exceed reasonably available hours," according to Sard, who concedes that she always feels there is too much to do and struggles with a conflict between work and personal time.

Many of the negative factors are typical of public interest work: inadequate secretarial, technical, or other support staff, and relatively low pay. Her position lacks status within the legal profession, Sard admits frankly, even though her work results in "helping families stay together, have a secure and decent place to live, and have more control over their own lives." The positives outweigh the negatives and keep her going.

> Despite its many frustrations in this era of increasingly mean-spirited politics and generally conservative decisionmakers, I am still convinced that there is no greater satisfaction and privilege than being able to use one's work hours and one's skills in efforts to help other people live a better life.

Nonprofit Organizations

The nonprofit sector of the economy offers thousands of opportunities for those with legal training who want to serve the legal needs of individuals. It is critical to recognize that the possibilities for employment go far beyond the approximately 900,000 organizations which have obtained tax-exempt status from the federal government. There are thousands of other agencies which might be interested in taking advantage of your law school skills.

The phrase that I like to use to describe these organizations is *advocacy*. Each has a fairly narrowly defined mission and related goals and objectives for which many who work there spend all or most of their time advocating. I like to use the word *advocacy* in connection with the attorneys who work in the nonprofit sector, too, because it is what your legal education should have trained you to do.

Putting that label on this world gives it the credibility perhaps needed when others question whether this is "an appropriate professional area for you" and when you yourself question whether you are qualified. It is interesting to note that the assumption of the former is that you are overqualified and the latter that you are underqualified. The truth is that it *is* an appropriate professional area and you *are* qualified.

By expanding your definition of nonprofits to include all those that have a defined mission and advocate for it, you open up a vast universe of about one and one-half million potential employers.

Types of Nonprofit Organizations

These organizations may be categorized initially by their settings, such as museums, schools and universities, libraries, theaters, historical landmarks, and other educational and cultural institutions.

There are foundations, charities, religious organizations, service groups, and organizations which promote research in the scientific field or another discipline. Many are national or international in scope with regional, state, or local chapters.

They can be grouped by their support of one or two target populations, such as those who serve the disabled, a particular ethnic group, children, the elderly, or abused women. Groups which serve the poor can be further distinguished by whether they help innercity residents or rural poor. There are organizations which serve a group of employees, such as a union, or a certain type of worker, such as a trade association or professional society. Thousands of associations or agencies are geared to help those afflicted with a particular disease or birth defect.

Nonprofits can be categorized by the one or two areas of social concern they focus on; for example, education, the environment, consumer issues, human rights, or government reform. The ideological positions may be in direct opposition, such as different groups involved in abortion issues, one which is pro-life and one which is pro-choice. Sometimes nonprofits with distinctly different philosophies work together on a common concern, such as a politically conservative group joining efforts of a welfare rights organization to change a system which neither group believes works effectively. For another look at nonprofit organizations, see the ABA Career Series book, *Nonlegal Careers for Lawyers,* Third Edition, Chapter 8, entitled "Associations and Institutions," American Bar Association, 1994.

Types of Positions within Nonprofits

There are a variety of ways attorneys work for nonprofit organizations depending on the size and mission of the organization. The staff position that automatically comes to mind may be that of in-house counsel or general counsel. Let's take a closer look at this position and some others within nonprofit organizations.

In-house Counsel or General Counsel—An attorney may be one of many in the nonprofit's legal department or the only lawyer handling the day-to-day legal issues which arise, such as worker's compensation, contracts, advising administrators, and preparing corporate documents.

The organization may hire legal staff with specific skills to handle non-litigation legal issues. For example, the Nature Conservancy, an organization that acquires and manages land, has staff attorneys who handle the legal and tax aspects of such ownership.

While the general public might associate a lawyer's role with going to court, litigation may take only a small fraction of the in-house counsel's time. If litigation is referred to an outside counsel, the nonprofit's legal counsel may act as overseer and liaison. Responsibilities may shift to reflect changing needs. Activities are varied and far from routine.

Unlike those in a private law firm, attorneys in nonprofit organizations have only one client. As a result they become more familiar with the organization's aims, may be involved in its short-range and long-term planning sessions, and generally have greater knowledge of both the organization and its area of concern.

Teaching, Writing, and Policy-Making—In addition to in-house counsel, attorneys are employed by nonprofits as writers, teachers, or policy-makers. They write or edit articles for newsletters, review legislation, draft grant proposals, testify before congressional committees, comment on proposed regulations, write booklets to explain laws for lay people, and write amicus briefs.

An attorney who works for an organization that seeks to effect changes in public policy or initiate law reform uses legal skills to advocate the organization's position. Activities may include research, analysis, policy development and advocacy; appellate court brief writing; writing educational materials; providing information or technical assistance to related organizations; proposing, drafting, and lobbying on state and federal agency rules and legislation; and monitoring government agency activities.

Management Positions—Management positions for lawyers within nonprofits might include communications director, department head, or executive director. The title of the position will vary as well as the particular responsibilities.

Nonprofit managers find themselves doing much of the same tasks as managers in the corporate world: planning, budgeting, and supervising people and projects. They may also become involved in working with volunteers, education and training, developing new programs or directions for the organization, and policy-making or legislative issues.

A communications director may write or coach the organization's president on a speech, news conference, or public appearance; supervise public relations activities, such as news releases; and oversee the nonprofit's publication program and promotional materials. The communications director may field queries from reporters working on a news story or direct them to the appropriate expert, and may respond to a reference in a story about an issue or the organization itself. The attorneys who work in this position for nonprofits work to build and maintain their credibility with reporters and serve as an important reference source on complex, fast-breaking stories.

The top manager in a nonprofit is generally referred to as the executive director or the chief executive officer (CEO.) This staff position is distinguished from the elected and generally voluntary position of president which may have a limited term of one or two years.

Sometimes an attorney who served as in-house or outside counsel moves into a management position because of the lawyer's extensive knowledge of the organization and the issues which concern it. Other times, a lawyer may be hired for a management position because he or she possesses other valuable experience or strengths and the legal skills are used in a supplemental but complimentary way. More and more nonprofits are looking to lawyers for management guidance because of the increasing complexity of issues that concern them and society itself.

One Lawyer's Experience Working with a Nonprofit Organization

Richard Bourne, a lawyer with Children's Hospital in Boston, consults with the professional staff—physicians, nurses, social workers, and psychologists—about the legal and ethical management of patient care issues such as informed consent, confidentiality, documentation, child abuse and domestic violence, withdrawal of care, duties to report to state or federal agencies, and admission and discharge matters. He also attends rounds and case conferences and communicates with police, district attorneys, DSS workers, and courts. His responsibilities include advising the hospital on employment problems and serving as a member of various committees, such as Safety, Risk Management, Ethics, AIDS Advisory, and Security. He drafts policies and procedures for the hospital and conducts in-hospital training sessions on medical-legal topics. He is always available by beeper for emergency response, e.g., obtaining a restraining order to prevent parents from removing a child from the facility.

Bourne believes his work meets his own goal of contributing to the individual and social good.

"I assist staff so that their work satisfies legal constraints while advancing patient interests," he explains. His position offers him autonomy, variety, sufficient income and security while providing him with the satisfaction of doing his job well.

"I don't know what emergent issues will arise during the work day," he says. "I might be involved in the issue of whether or not a child should receive treatment that the medical team deems 'futile,' but that family is demanding."

Like many who work for a nonprofit or any large organization, Bourne finds interpersonal and "political" skills are key and describes them as important as legal knowledge and analysis.

"Physicians in a hierarchical organization may not welcome legal input, seeing it as an infringement on medical turf," he says. "I have to accomplish my legal goals in a way that is not provocative and causes the staff to view me as a support rather than a hindrance."

Many times, Bourne has had to accept that his role has its boundaries in the hospital setting; the lawyer should not "play" clinician. He may limit his role to presenting an analysis, the costs and benefits of various alternatives, rather than giving a conclusion or pretending that the legal perspective is "truth" or the only appropriate orientation.

This sometimes means allowing others to take credit, he adds, working behind the scenes or indirectly to effect an outcome. "The ego needs to be constrained," he explains, "and becomes so if one is secure in both one's person and one's role."

His work demands that he remain cool no matter what the crisis is, maintaining the ability to think things through despite a panic situation, time constraints, and the seriousness of the decision being made.

His advice to law students includes the following:

> Know yourself and try to find a position that fits with your interests and skills. Don't accept dollars or a title because of what your parents advocate or because society defines these factors as valuable. In whatever position you accept, learn as much as you can, fully 'drink' the experience, and try to focus on the strengths and benefits rather than the costs. Be flexible, and if you really hate what you're doing, leave because life is too short to do otherwise, but scout out alternatives before you leap. Remember that, despite life being too short, it is also long. Mistakes are inevitable, sadness heals with time, and process is as important as substance.

Bourne also advises law students to integrate pleasure and work to the extent possible.

> Remember that doing for others—making a contribution to individuals and to society—and personal relationships are important to one's satisfaction and happiness with life, but you also need enough money so that you're not always worrying about bills and have sufficient freedom of choice to take an occasional vacation or buy rollerblades.

Private Law Firms

By far the greatest number of openings for those who want to use traditional adversarial skills to work on behalf of individuals or to serve the public employing the traditional court-oriented approach are in private law firms.

You have to disregard the widespread myth that says that public interest practice and private law practice are mutually exclusive terms. Such a distinction probably arose as a form of guilt-salving within academia and the legal profession. As the embarrassment grew over the effectiveness of the funneling of law students away from public service into big firms, schools and law firms began to encourage law students and lawyers to do *pro bono* work; i.e., to make sacrifices for a short time to help the poor. Such an approach should be ignored because it is based on the assumption that serving the public is an extracurricular activity on the road to becoming a partner, not the basis for a long-term career helping individuals.

In addition, as a practical matter, this country has not provided resources or financial incentives sufficient to lead to the creation of public entities to represent those most in need of services. It is important to recognize that out of approximately 806,000 lawyers, only about 10,000 practice with the public law firms which include the Legal Services offices, public defender programs, and public interest litigation organizations described above. About 73%, or 587,000 lawyers, are in private practice.

The average size of a private law firm in this country is 1.8 lawyers and 44.7% of all lawyers in private practice or 262,500 attorneys are solo practitioners. Almost two-thirds (65%) are in firms of five or less lawyers! (Barbara A. Curran and Clara N. Carson, *The Lawyer Statistical Report: The U.S. Legal Profession in the 1990s,* American Bar Foundation, 1994.) You need to be aware of where there are substantial numbers of lawyers involved because that is where there is the greatest likelihood of finding an opening.

A superb sampling of such firms can be found in the 1993–1994 *National Lawyers Guild's National Referral Directory.* The National Lawyers Guild (NLG) is an association of lawyers and legal workers whose stated aim is to bring together those

> who recognize the importance of safeguarding and extending the rights of workers, women, farmers, and minority groups upon whom the welfare of the entire nation depends; who seek actively to eliminate racism; who work to maintain and protect our civil rights and liberties in the face of persistent attacks upon them, and who look upon the law as an instrument for the protection of the people, rather than for their repression. (Preamble to the NLG Constitution)

Private practices usually do not have either the legislative and regulatory restraints of Legal Services offices and public defenders nor the mission statement of the public interest litigation organizations to limit or guide their caseload. Lawyers who start their own practice do so with different levels of experience, do not generally think about a "marketing" approach or defining their "product," and tend to take the cases that come through the door. They gain experience in a few areas sufficient to take up most of their time.

A reading of the NLG directory shows how difficult it is to pigeonhole private practices into simple categories. Some may take cases in employment law, civil rights, tort litigation, immigration, family law and consumer issues. Some represent individuals in family, landlord-tenant, personal injury, job-related injuries, social security disability, estates and wills. Others that describe a practice as employment law (worker's compensation, social security, occupational safety, discrimination, wrongful termination), are easier to categorize.

But being a solo practitioner or attorney in a small firm doesn't rule out practicing public interest law or only doing work in this area on a *pro bono* basis. Thousands of small firm practitioners accept cases every day on behalf of clients who are neither indigent nor wealthy but have a "personal plight" legal issue.

Say for example you want to devote your time to women's rights, but there is only one Women's Rights Law Center. Short of starting your own institution what can you do?

You can practice in a recognized related area, in this case family, domestic relations and divorce, where you can be involved in and have continuous contact with your area of primary concern. Women's rights in the workplace are the focus of plaintiff employment discrimination practitioners and firms working on behalf of employees and unions.

Suppose your interests are in the area of criminal law. Rather than view your options as limited to either the prosecutors' or public defenders' offices, expand your search to the vast criminal defense bar.

Similarly, environmental law may be the focus of only a few public interest litigation organizations in your state, but there are hundreds of law firms who litigate on behalf of individuals in the area of toxic tort and lead paint as part of a caseload which includes other products liability and personal injury cases.

Burton A. Nadler is a private practitioner who describes his work as advising and representing individuals and groups in the areas of landlord/tenant law ("single-room-only tenants against a slumlord for decrepit conditions and rent gouging"); election law ("for rent control advocates and 'left' candidates involved in electoral politics"); personal injury ("lead paint poisoning of a child"); employment law ("sexual harassment"); worker's compensation ("after falling from a scaffolding"); civil rights ("discrimination based on race, gender, and sexual preference in employment and housing.")

Nadler's typical day is like that of any other private practitioner, drafting letters, interviewing new clients, meeting with staff on maintaining case flow management, and preparing for trial, but he believes his work enables him "to see a slight glimmer of social justice for clients that would otherwise never see even a flicker" from the legal system.

"Be it protecting rent control, pursuing sexual harassment claims, or advising nonprofit organizations, the opportunity to feel good about my work is important," he says. "I also really like the people I work with; they give me a semblance of balance in an otherwise hostile world of lawyers."

Nadler uses his legal skills to conceptualize solutions for his clients and build consensus, often settling or "cajoling to seek a middle ground," rather than fight a battle through the court system which would not ultimately benefit anyone, least of all his clients. He advises students to develop conflict resolution skills and reminds them that "there is much more to life than money."

3
A Career Path

Over the last thirty years I have read workday accounts of numerous lawyers and student interns, solicited and distributed hundreds of others, and had the opportunity to talk with many law school graduates who followed the path created by their hopes, values, and concerns. They have found excitement, career satisfaction, and fulfillment serving individuals and the public. Some of their comments and quotes appear throughout this book.

The truth is that career paths are seldom as linear as we often imagine them to be. Finding the position that satisfies your goals takes time and effort. As you grow, professionally and personally, your goals and your work may evolve.

Catherine Steane, a 1984 graduate of Yale Law School, relates her own experience as an illustration of this. Her personal account updating an article which appeared in *Yale Law Graduates at Work* follows.

Catherine Steane: Before and during law school, I wanted to practice public interest law. When I didn't obtain a clerkship or fellowship, finances dictated that I sign up with a large corporate firm. I worked downtown, at two different firms, for two years and hated every minute of it. I had no free time, the stress left me in bad health, there was an enormous incongruity between the people I worked with and the kind of people I wanted to spend my time with, and I got no sense of self-worth from my work.

After two years, I decided there was simply no reason to be so miserable and conducted a broad, though blessedly brief, search for a public interest job. I got all of my best leads through my softball team. The lesson in that is, when you're looking for a job, let everyone in the world know you're looking because the good leads will come from the sources you least expect.

I found a position in a private firm with one principal and two other associates representing tenants threatened with eviction and bringing wrongful eviction lawsuits for tenants evicted without "just cause." My clients represented the city's diversity in terms of race, sex, ethnicity, sexual orientation, age, education, and income. The ability to handle affirmative suits on a contingent basis allowed us to represent low-income people who could not otherwise afford to pay for a lawyer.

In a typical week I would consult with clients in person or over the phone, appear in court for a motion or a settlement conference, take or defend a deposition, draft pleadings and motions, talk to opposing counsel over the phone, propound and respond to discovery, and write letters. Actual trials were rare because of our success as negotiators, the pressure on insurance carriers to settle because of the potential exposure, and the inability of many clients to finance a trial on an hourly basis.

I handled my cases largely by myself, making most of the tactical decisions, yet consulting with my boss on almost every case. Thus, I received two kinds of training—direct advice on how to do things and the experience of having to make decisions myself.

I loved my job. I never worked weekends. I had a pleasant work environment and a great deal of autonomy and responsibility without feeling that I had been cast to sea without a life preserver. My work was an extension of my political beliefs and I got a great deal of satisfaction from the feeling that I provided needed, high quality services to people in crisis. I found the substantive work interesting and challenging. I didn't get paid enough, making about half of what my downtown peers were making, but more than traditional public interest jobs and enough to make ends meet.

What I learned as a part of the "plaintiffs' bar" is that there are lots of jobs out there not in the traditional public interest agency mold where one can do good works for everyday people and still make a reasonable living. In California, at least, there are ample opportunities for private attorneys to make a living representing plaintiffs in employment law, insurance bad faith, products liability, and medical malpractice, to name a few fields.

After about two years in that small firm, I set up my own practice, continuing to specialize in housing rights. I later added wills, powers of attorney, and relationship agreements to my repertoire, as these are much in demand in my community.

Solo practice is prodigiously hard work. In addition to practicing a lot of law, one must set up and manage an office; hire, supervise and fire personnel; be a business getter and a bill collector; and make wise decisions about purchasing equipment, furniture, supplies, and contractual services. One can never rest; there is always more to do. It is exceptionally difficult to take vacations and impossible to be sick.

But you are free to pursue whatever opportunities you want. As long as you are willing to take the financial consequences, you don't have to take on cases or clients you don't like. I took the opportunity to pursue some pro bono work that I probably would not have been free to do had I been working for someone else. I was able to make a significant contribution to the legal response to San Francisco's devastating earthquake. I was able to write a guide on eliminating sexual orientation discrimination in the legal workplace that was published and disseminated nationwide by the Bar Association of San Francisco. I was able to participate for three years in the screening of candidates for appointment to the bench.

The greatest reward of solo practice is the enormous sense of accomplishment that comes from creating something out of nothing: making one's own opportunities, providing a service to the community that would not otherwise exist, creating employment and business for your support staff and contractors. Solo practice is the fondest dream and worst nightmare of a control queen: you get to make all the decisions, but you have absolutely no control over where the next piece of business is going to come from. It is impossible to predict or control your financial future. And all the hard work in the world might not be rewarded; a downturn in the economy, a change in the law in your practice area, or a bad business judgment can steal the fruits of your labor at any time.

One day I realized I wasn't having any fun *and* I wasn't making any money. One should always be doing at least one, if not both.

I was also simply lonely. I didn't share office space with other attorneys, which is one way many solos avoid isolation. I closed down my practice and accepted a position with a city attorney's office, a good place to be for people who want to do trials but don't want to do criminal law. The pay was good and the hours were reasonable. Some cases were more interesting than others. The quality of practice varies. It was sometimes, but not always, difficult to believe that one was on the right side of the case. It was a very social, but politically treacherous, office. After being laid off in a budget crisis, and devoting five months to looking hard for work in a terrible market, I was graced with the kind of job I went to law school for: a staff attorney position with a national nonprofit public interest organization. While I have not yet been there long enough to describe the experience at length, I can make a couple of observations.

The first is that one should not romanticize what it is like to work at a nonprofit. There are similarities in the dynamics of every workplace. Income has to be brought in, work has to be churned out, and personalities and politics have to be dealt with.

The second is that, for all the similarities to the for-profit scene, it makes a world of difference to work every day on things that matter, on things designed to make the world a better place in a significant way. It took me nine difficult years to get here, but I couldn't ask for more job satisfaction.

Find Your Own Career Path

Steane, like others who use their law degree to serve others, has found her own job satisfaction by doing so. The career path you choose may not be straight and narrow, and it may not be the one others have envisioned for you. But if you set your own goals and listen to the voice within, you will never be lost. You may be like the 1979 law school graduate who has been representing migrant farm workers since law school and told me he was the happiest person at his tenth reunion.

4

Setting Your Goals

With all the possibilities mentioned in Chapter 2 you should understand by now that there are many ways to avoid becoming as dissatisfied and disillusioned as those attorneys referred to in the introductory chapter. To find a truly satisfying career, it is wise to master some career planning fundamentals first.

One book I highly recommend in this area is *What Color Is Your Parachute?*, a popular guide to finding the ideal career written by Richard Bolles. (Ten Speed Press, Berkeley, CA, 1994) Bolles's book is geared to general audiences and law students might find Gary Munneke's *The Legal Career Guide: From Law Student to Lawyer* and *Lawyers in Transition* by Mark L. Byers to be more valuable.

The purpose of career planning is to enable you to map out a development plan for your career, not simply "find a job," as Munneke says. It means taking an active role in choosing your options rather than allowing yourself to be "placed" somewhere.

Because planning is so fundamental to obtaining professional satisfaction, I have borrowed from these books and drawn from my own career counseling experience to outline four key principles of career planning.

1. Your primary goal must be personal workplace satisfaction.

"Life is too short to spend it being miserable," Munneke points out in his book *The Legal Career Guide: From Law Student to Lawyer* (ABA Law Student Division Career Series, 1992). There are plenty of unhappy lawyers out there, as the surveys quoted in the introductory chapter reveal. Remember: 66–70% of the lawyers would take another job if they had the opportunity. Lawyers who "fall into" a career rut rather than consciously choose to follow a particular career path are the ones who later end up describing their work as tedious and meaningless. Munneke illustrates this principle with a story of a law student who works on a bankruptcy case during a summer internship, takes a job with a firm after graduation and handles another bankruptcy case, and before long is designated as the firm "bankruptcy attorney." The only problem is that he hates bankruptcy.

Bolles puts it another way in his book:

> Suppose your strongest and most favorable skills involve welding....Do you want to weld together a wheel or do want to weld the casing of a nuclear bomb?...You are starting here at exactly the opposite place from where most job-hunters begin. They begin with vacancies...They let the vacancies call the shots for their life....You are starting with the issue of where you would like to work. Later you can inquire whether or not there are ... jobs. But you begin with the high energy and excitement generated (inevitably) by your dreams.
>
> Bolles, *What Color Is your Parachute?*

2. You must select an employment option which is consistent with your personal and professional goals.

Career planning professionals have for years taught law students that the recognition and pursuit of their goals and values is an integral part of the search for workplace satisfaction. In addition, the 1993 ABA report of the Task Force on Law Schools and the Profession, commonly referred to as the "MacCrate Report," lists as one of the legal profession's fundamental values the following:

> As a member of a learned profession, a lawyer should be committed to the value of selecting and maintaining employment that will allow the lawyer to develop as a professional and to pursue his or her professional and personal goals.

In its recommendations, the Task Force told law schools that it is just as important that their students learn such values as it is to acquire substantive knowledge. The report also concluded that whether a lawyer develops professional goals in law school or elsewhere, it is the individual's obligation to ensure that the position taken is consistent with his or her own professional and personal goals.

If you do not have a clear vision of what your personal and professional goals are, there are several ways to explore them. The law school probably offers several classes which touch upon professionalism and ethics. Many of the career planning books, including those by Byers, Arron, Bolles, and Munneke, contain exercises like the one which follows later in this chapter to help you identify goals. Your academic advisor or a personal mentor should also be asked to help you sort out what you want to do with your legal training. A part-time job or summer experience may lead to other discoveries.

Keep in mind that your goals may differ from those of your parents, your classmates, or your colleagues. The key is to make sure your goals are ones you can live with.

I remember a classmate, in one of my reunion books, relating how he heard the "word"—what it meant to be a man—from a peasant sitting at the side of a road in Central America. Now, after 25 years using these words to guide his life, he realized they made no sense. He couldn't believe that for most of his adult life, he had, without analysis, pursued a path laid out by someone he did not know who was sitting in an isolated corner of the world.

As foolish as this seems, it really is no different than the thousands of graduating students who accept a job based on the salary offered and then discover at the age of 35 or 45 or 55 that money is not everything.

3. You must be aware of how the law school experience diverts students from these goals.

It is ironic that while offering discussions on professional goals, the law school process itself instills the opposite values in students. Even though an estimated 40% of law students start out wanting a career that strives for social justice or helping those who need help, only a small fraction, maybe 5%, actually accept a position upon graduation that will enable them to do so. As Munneke warns:

> Law school will give new meaning to the word challenge. From the law school you attend, to your class rank, to your extra-curricular activities, to your work experience, everything and everyone will seem to conspire to stand between you and the job you want. (*The Legal Career Guide: From Law Student to Lawyer*, p. 78)

Since your goal is not to find a job in which you are likely to become quickly disillusioned and dissatisfied, you have to do more than devote all your time to doing classwork and learning "how to think like a lawyer." Use those sharply honed analytical skills to scrutinize whatever "common wisdom" you hear about legal career options in the classroom, the corridors, and the dining room.

Although this book is not intended to be a comprehensive critique of the law schools, because of the absolute predictability of the diversion of law students from the careers described in it, any guide which purports to provide advice to you in this area would be of limited use and superficial if it did not point out the many obstacles you will encounter along the way. The law school community erects, consciously or unconsciously, many barriers and pressures that often affect how you and others think and act. These are powerful influences filled with invalid assumptions about the practice of law in general and public interest law careers in particular.

For example, Professor David Chambers noted in a report to Dean Lee Bollinger of the University of Michigan School of Law that while some students perceive the faculty as actively encouraging students to enter large-firm practice or as actively denigrating work in government or public defenders offices, "a more accurate single characterization of the general faculty attitude would be inattention, of very limited conscious involvement in guiding the career choices of our students." He suggests that more faculty members should become involved in encouraging students to consider small firms, government, legal services or public interest work.

> Of the five-year alumni who do remember beginning law school with long-term plans, about a third remember hoping to work in government, legal services or public interest work. By the end of law school, many fewer retained such long-term plans .... (P)erhaps with effort, the faculty can have an impact in shaping the plans of those who arrive without plans and in strengthening the resolve of those who arrive hoping for a career in government or service to low-income clients. Exactly what sorts of faculty efforts might work we cannot be certain. We can envision ... faculty members arranging more class sessions to which practitioners in a field are invited; and, more broadly, faculty members simply trying harder to convey to our students from the beginning of their first year that we have a genuine interest in what they do with their lives.

In addition, in his 1990 report entitled *Public Loss* Jaron Bourque notes that the atmosphere at many law schools "discourages students from reflecting upon the societal implications of their course work. First year curricula at most schools often do not emphasize such reflection. Law schools rarely encourage students to think critically about their future careers and plan accordingly." Bourque criticizes law schools which "have narrowly defined their responsibility for providing lawyers to all members of society." He writes:

> Even the most progressive schools have promoted public interest law careers in a piecemeal fashion. While critical, career development resources for students with little experience with public interest causes is insufficient, since counseling alone cannot persuade students to forgo positions in prestigious large firms and their large starting salaries.

4. You must be prepared to take control over, and personal responsibility for, the decision-making on all issues which vitally concern your career and your life.

Munneke defines the underlying concept of self-determination when he states, "Too many are willing to give up their self-respect by handing over the power to make decisions about their lives to others."

In other words, unless you are willing to take control over your life and your career, unless you are willing to make the decisions about such important issues in your life, you are likely to find yourself in a situation which can be defined as either "your worst personal nightmare" or "someone else's dream for you."

Whatever position you take combines many goals and values, some desired and some unwanted. Whether or not you are an active participant in the process, you will eventually find yourself in a job—the result of decisions you make. You will have "chosen" the outcome, consciously or unconsciously. Remember the adage, "Not to decide is to decide." If you default on this professional obligation, you have decided to be "placed" somewhere based on the needs and criteria of others. The choice is up to you.

An Exercise to Explore Your Personal and Professional Goals

Looking at the list of items on page 32, check off *all* those you would like to have in your ideal workplace. Be inclusive, not selective, so that you have checked off at least 20 items by the time you finish. If you have more than that, eliminate those with the lowest priority to reduce the number to twenty.

Next evaluate your most recent work experience (paid or volunteer, law or non-law) in light of your ideal workplace. Place a number from 0 to 5 next to each item checked representing the degree that item was satisfied in that position, a "5" indicates complete satisfaction, a "2" or "3" indicates partial satisfaction and a "0" means that characteristic was not found in the workplace. When you have finished, add up the numbers. It should not come as a surprise that the highest possible score is 100.

This exercise has been given to lawyers and used by law students to rate summer or part-time work experiences. The results reflect how satisfying their work has been. Lawyers and law students with very rewarding experiences will have scores in the 80s and 90s. A partner in a New York law firm scored 6—yes, 6—on a scale of 100, including 0s for self-respect and self-confidence! Obviously, she and her position are not a good match. Likewise those whose scores are in the 30s or the 40s know they are generally dissatisfied.

Characteristics and Goals in Your Ideal Workplace

Step 1: Place a check to the left of all the items below and on page 33 which you would like to have in your ideal workplace. Make sure you have at least 20 items by the time you finish. If you have more than 20, eliminate those with the lowest priority.

Step 2: Evaluate your most recent work experience in light of your ideal workplace. Place a number from 0—5 in the column to the right of each checked item representing the degree to which that characteristic was found in your latest experience. A "5" indicates complete satisfaction, a "2" or "3" indicates partial satisfaction, and "0" indicates the ideal characteristic was not found.

Step 3: Add up the numbers. The highest possible score is 100. Those generally satisfied with their work experience score in the 80s or 90s and those dissatisfied score somewhere in the 30s and 40s.

My ideal workplace: **My most recent work experience:**

(Check 20 items)   (Rate checked items 0-5)

____ Offers an opportunity to work with a team   ____

____ Provides intellectual stimulation   ____

____ Rewards competition   ____

____ Presents opportunities to be creative   ____

____ Allows time to do non-career activities   ____

____ Creates a comfortable atmosphere for self-expression   ____

____ Offers job security   ____

____ Provides financial security   ____

____ Includes public recognition   ____

____ Provides opportunity to be with friends and family   ____

____ Contributes to self-respect and self-esteem   ____

____ Promotes self-confidence   ____

____ Offers the chance to work with people I like   ____

____ Includes involvement with important social issues   ____

____ Provides a variety of responsibilities   ____

_____ Offers opportunities to assert power and influence   _____

_____ Provides opportunities to learn and improve skills   _____

_____ Allows time to spend on personal matters   _____

_____ Includes direct contact with individuals   _____

_____ Involves work consistent with values and beliefs   _____

_____ Affirms belief in rightness of client's cause   _____

_____ Contributes to the public good   _____

_____ Tolerates cultural and ethnic diversity   _____

_____ Accommodates need to be comfortable in dress   _____

_____ Discourages actions which "hurt" others   _____

_____ Offers a significant amount of autonomy   _____

_____ Minimizes clerical work   _____

_____ Satisfies aversion to institutions and hierarchy   _____

_____ Includes living in preferred geographic location   _____

_____ Provides opportunity to travel   _____

_____ Requires long hours   _____

_____ Affirms importance of bringing about social change   _____

_____ Offers opportunity to do something that matters   _____

_____ Offers opportunity to feel needed   _____

_____ Develops skills through training with close supervision   _____

_____ Provides opportunity for immediate responsibility   _____

_____ Meets need to be involved in the decision-making process   _____

_____ Offers chance to work in a small growing organization   _____

_____ Provides trial experience as soon as possible   _____

_____ Meets need to feel "good" about one's work   _____

_____ Meets need to be involved and accomplish things   _____

Total Score: _____

Workplace satisfaction is an objective made up of your personal and professional goals. Remember that you have the ability to be an active participant in the process and can "choose" to have a 20 or an 85. Take control.

Frequently Cited Goals

Some of the goals and values of public interest lawyers are revealed in their descriptions of the work they do. These goals may be broadly grouped into two professional goals, "Providing Service to Others" and "Increasing Knowledge and Skills." The two most frequently cited personal goals are "Working in a Compatible Environment" and "Having Autonomy."

Professional Goal Number 1
Providing Service to Others

The importance of serving others is apparent in the number of times these lawyers refer to this aspect of their work. Many describe their work as having "a substantial impact on people's lives," "contributing to the individual and social good," or "doing something meaningful."

Attorneys stress the value of improving the legal system when they talk about "promoting justice," "providing people with an opportunity to seek justice," or "working to accomplish policy changes." Their version of this goal may be loosely defined as "advancing the public good" or "providing high quality services to people in crisis," but their feeling is that they can make a difference and is closely related to career satisfaction. They derive satisfaction from the fact that their work "makes the world a better place." For those who help the underprivileged and underrepresented daily, work is an extension of their political beliefs, not just an occasional experience.

Professional Goal Number 2
Increasing Knowledge and Gaining Skills

The lawyers who refer to their cases as "exciting," "complex," and "intellectually challenging" are never bored. They are constantly learning new things and improving their skills. The diversity of their caseloads is revealed in descriptive phrases such as "never routine" and "no typical days."

Despite the challenges of "perpetual crises," being able to resolve problems creates a feeling of accomplishment and builds self-confidence. Having opportunities to learn, using one's unique skills and creativity, gaining trial experience, and working directly with individuals is stimulating and contributes greatly to career satisfaction.

Personal Goal Number 1
Working in a Compatible Environment

Also critical to personal satisfaction is the comfort employees feel in their surroundings. Lawyers who describe their office as having a "wonderful atmosphere," "supportive colleagues," or "shared commitment" enjoy their work much more. A compatible environment includes achieving a balance of work and family, allowing for cultural and ethnic diversity, and providing a comfortable place for self-expression. Some organizations offer employees self-respect, self-esteem, and self-worth, which are just as important as providing a sufficient income for them. Feeling comfortable can include everything from "liking those people I work with" to "good hours" to "being able to work in jeans." Those who see the workplace as friendly and supportive are much happier about the hours they spend in the office.

Personal Goal Number 2
Having Autonomy

The ability to have a significant and meaningful role in the work accomplished is one of the keys to personal satisfaction. Lawyers unhappy with their jobs often gripe that they have no control over their work or that every task is subject to someone else's input and approval. "I was told to put off an important hearing on one case to work for a partner 'or it would not look good,'" one attorney in a large firm complained. Those who feel someone is constantly watching over their shoulder see it as an indication of lack of confidence.

Being autonomous and working for a large organization are not mutually exclusive, although many find it easier to find independence working in a small organization or for oneself. Those who have an aversion to hierarchies and institutional constraints where pressure to conform can be strong would do well to seek employment elsewhere.

Having independence and responsibility, being one's own boss or at least being significantly involved in the decision-making process are considered part of being a professional and increase personal satisfaction.

What Are Your Goals?

Your own goals may vary from those mentioned here or include others, but this chapter should serve as a starting point for defining your goals. If service to others, an intellectual challenge, autonomy, and a comfortable workplace environment are significant workplace criteria for you, do not abandon them. It is true that all places have their pros and cons, but do not let anyone minimize the impact of being in a situation every day where your work is not consistent with your personal and professional goals.

Career satisfaction can be identified by the simple phrase "I love my job." Thousands of lawyers have found workplace satisfaction by trusting and believing in themselves. You can, too.

5
Finding Your Way

Finding your way to a satisfying career that meets your personal and professional goals takes time and effort. Law students who begin exploring options and narrowing their search while still in school have an advantage over those who wait until after graduation. Similarly, those who begin in their first year have an advantage over those who start planning their careers in the second or third year.

It has often been said "Finding a job is a full time job." This can be particularly daunting when your time is already allocated to law school studies or a full time job elsewhere. If you make your efforts a genuine priority and not an extracurricular "hobby," you can expect to spend about the same amount of time planning your career that you would devote to a single law course. If you divide your planning and career search efforts into tasks that can be accomplished throughout your years at school, you will find them much more manageable and less overwhelming.

Should devoting this much time to something when you are already so busy seem impossible, consider the alternative: being "placed" somewhere, *anywhere,* upon graduation because the position is open and you are available. While placement is infinitely easier in the short run, it may ultimately lead to dissatisfaction with your job. Keep in mind that more than two-thirds of lawyers would switch jobs tomorrow given the opportunity.

The alternative, self-directed approach is much more likely to result in a professionally and personally rewarding career. Therefore the career planning process should be viewed as being integral to your legal education and once you begin incorporating the necessary steps into your workload, you will find the benefits equal to the amount of time and effort expended.

The Career Choice and the Job Search Processes

There are two stages in Munneke's analysis of professional development—the career choice process and the job search process—

and it is fundamental that the first must precede the second. In other words, you have to know what you are looking for if you expect to find it.

This chapter summarizes Munneke's career choice and job search processes while adapting them for those pursuing careers serving the legal needs of the public, but law students may find it helpful to refer to the full text in *The Career Planning Guide: From Law Student to Lawyer.* (ABA Law Student Division Career Series, 1992.)

The Career Choice Process

In the first year of law school, you learn about the options, the settings included within the definition of careers serving the legal needs of the public, such as private law firms, public law firms and non-profit organizations. At the same time you will be encouraged to recognize the importance of selecting a workplace for not only that summer, but eventually a full-time position that is consistent with your personal and professional goals.

During the second year, you begin to analyze your skills. Through courses, extracurricular activities, term-time and summer work, you increase your knowledge and you improve your skills. You will also continue to explore all your options, evaluate the market for lawyers in the areas that appeal to you, and by the end of the second summer, you will rank your options and establish priorities.

The Job Search Process

The search for a particular job which fulfills your goals begins in your last year. Munneke divides the job search into five steps: packaging yourself, researching potential employers, building a network, selling yourself, and making a decision.

Keep in mind that you are not undertaking this effort just to find a position at graduation. You will use it every time you are ready to move onto a new job and you are likely to make that transition at least five times during your career. At every juncture of your career, you should evaluate the prior workplace experience and repeat some parts of the cycle as you search for a new position.

As you consciously move from one position to another, you will be creating a meaningful and unique history—your own career path. With that in mind, let's take a closer look at how you go about the career choice and job search processes, beginning with the first year of law school.

6
Exploring Options

Ideally, you should spend considerable time your first year of law school exploring the wide variety of options available to those who have a law degree. If you are approaching graduation or already have a legal position, you may be aware of many of those options, but you may also have encountered some opinions which would deter you from choosing them. Try to keep an open mind. What "conventional wisdom" might advise may not be what you want to do with your life.

In exploring your options, be sure to look at possibilities that are not considered traditional legal positions. You may have particular talents or skills and choose to use your degree in a supplementary way. As the MacCrate Report stated:

> In order to find employment that is consistent with his or her profes-
> sional goals and personal values, a lawyer must be familiar with the
> range of traditional and non-traditional employment opportunities for
> lawyers. (MacCrate, p. 220)

Once you are aware of the variety of options, the next step is to devote much of the remainder of the first year to finding out what it is like to practice in an area of interest in one of these categories. The MacCrate Report confirmed the importance of finding out beforehand what it might be like to practice a particular kind of law.

> Greater knowledge of what lawyers do in the various sectors of prac-
> tice can be useful to ... the law graduate in helping him or her to
> seek employment compatible with the lawyer's interests and aptitude.
> (MacCrate, p. 35)

But how do you find out what it is like, for example, to practice criminal law in a public defender's office? How can you know what it might mean to be a family lawyer in a small private law firm prac-tice and whether you might enjoy it or hate it?

You might take a clinical course and practice in that area. Or you might take a traditional course from someone who has practiced in that field. Find out what is offered by the career planning and placement office at your school or nearby law schools. Many schedule workshops featuring panels of practicing lawyers who can offer a realistic view of the field and also become valuable contacts.

Another way to learn about a particular field is to take a summer job, part-time job, work as a volunteer, or seek an internship in that area. If you want to learn more about housing discrimination, for example, you could work during the school year either for pay or in an internship in the state agency that files discrimination complaints.

The least enlightening approach to finding out about what it is like to practice in an area may be by reading about it but, unfortunately, because of the absence of other options, this is what many students must rely on. It may be difficult, for example, to really find out what immigration law entails because your school might not offer such a course or because there are so few summer jobs available to law students in this area.

Your first stop for learning about the resources available to you should be the Career Services Office (CSO) where most of the resources listed in Chapter 9 and Appendix 1, as well as other locally developed useful material, are likely to be found. In addition, many law schools have changed the manner in which they serve students seeking opportunities with organizations other than those who traditionally interview at the schools (large law firms). Some schools have hired a separate counselor (not part of the CSO) with public interest experience to assist students pursuing public interest options. Other schools have designated one member of the CSO staff as a public interest adviser. Depending on the law school, you can also learn about resources from other CSO counseling staff, representatives of your National Association for Public Interest Law (NAPIL) organization and the National Lawyers Guild Chapter, and the local representative of Pro Bono Students America.

To begin to learn more about the various options you might read "Day in the Life" accounts of lawyers. Your CSO may have surveyed its alumni/ae and placed the responses in a three-ring binder or published it, i.e.; *Yale Law Graduates at Work, Alumni/ae in Action* (Harvard Law School Office of Public Interest Advising). You might also refer to the evaluations that students have written about positions they have held during the summer or term-time. These may be compiled by your law school or, if it is part of a regional consortium of the Pro Bono Students America, you will have access to the evaluations completed by those who have found positions through that program. The *NAPIL Summer Internship Directory* also contains a number of student evaluations.

Check with your CSO for a new guide recently published by the ABA, entitled *Law School Public Interest Law Support Programs: A Directory*. This resource lists a range of public interest programs available to law students, such as fellowships and summer internships, student organizations, law journals, manadatory pro bono requirements, voluntary pro bono opportunities, specialized career services, and clinical programs. For further information or to purchase a copy, write Elissa C. Lichtenstein, Public Service Division, American Bar Association, 740 15th Street NW, Ninth Floor, Washington, DC 20005.

While there are many stories about lawyers in national legal periodicals such as the *National Law Journal* and the *American Lawyer* and regional publications such as the *Massachusetts Lawyers Weekly,* you certainly do not need to limit yourself to them. For many of you, the O.J. Simpson trial itself may be the source of a lifetime of reading in the popular press. There are a wealth of books and articles by and about lawyers in the CSO, the law school library, and your nearby paperback bookstore.

And on a Computer Near You . . .

How can you use the computer to find out more about options? Ask the CSO and the law school law library staff about the computerized databases and on-line services provided by Lexis, Nexis and Westlaw, how to obtain an ID number and technical questions about their use. Alumni/ae should contact the local office of both companies for details about the services available to them. Both companies have useful resources for identifying and exploring public interest positions.

Lexis provides access to *Martindale-Hubbell* (a lawyer to lawyer reference book listing attorneys nationwide with biographical information, law school attended, firm affiliation, and areas of practice concentration); *United States Government Manual* (descriptions of all federal agencies, including field offices and the names of the department heads); and *Mentor File* (publications providing information about networking, marketing, and law firm management strategies, including *How to Start and Build a Law Practice* and *Non-Traditional Jobs Where You Can Use a Law Degree.*

Nexis (a component of Lexis) provides on-line access to numerous legal and general periodicals including both print and video media (transcripts of programs). It is possible to search for the names of both individuals and organizations, government agencies, corporations and law firms mentioned in the press and historical information.

Westlaw provides access to West's Legal Directory databases (information about lawyers in a variety of settings including government, academia and corporations—names, addresses, telephone number, areas of practice, date of birth, current position and length of time in that position), legal periodicals and general and legal newspapers; current and historical information about individuals and organizations; practice areas (thousands of databases useful in finding information about particular areas of legal practice of interest to you).

In addition to these on-line services helpful information is available on a number of other on-line services. Every day there are articles about individuals using the computer as part of their career and job search. While the most obvious examples of career related information are job listings such as the E-Span Interactive Employment Network and Career Mosaic on the Internet, at this point you will want to take advantage of resources that allow you to explore options, perhaps profiling law firms and non-profit organizations. You might read articles available on CompuServe or do research on the Internet.

You will also want to communicate with other lawyers and law students. There are many ways to do so without making a "cold call" which might be inconvenient for the attorney. Ask if your CSO has contacted alumni/ae and asked them to be "mentors." If there is such a list, do not hesitate to contact them. It is likely that they are underused, rather than burdened by law students contacting them.

Here again the computer may be useful. Lexis' Martindale-Hubbell and West's Legal Directory databases can be searched to find graduates of your law school who concentrate in civil rights, family, toxic torts, criminal defense, employee rights, immigration, etc. Join a forum or usernet group in which law students or lawyers participate on CompuServe, Prodigy, America On-Line, or the Internet.

There are other ways of contacting lawyers within a particular field. You probably know many people who know others with ties to a certain area. Think about family members, friends and neighbors, present and former colleagues or employers, lawyers you have met, law school classmates, your undergraduate career services office, and staff members of organizations to which you belong.

Once you have discovered someone who practices in a particular area, contact the attorney with an informal note or letter expressing your interest and asking if you might discuss the field with him or her sometime. In your note, explain that you are not looking for a job, but would like to learn more about that field and would appreciate thirty minutes of his or her time.

The aim of the discussion is to gain information to help you evaluate this particular career choice in terms of your goals and your skills. Plan to do at least two such informational interviews in each area that interests you.

When you meet with the attorney, have your questions prepared. What are the responsibilities of the position? What experience and training would be relevant? Which needed skills do you lack? What is the economic outlook for the area? Are there organizations that do similar work? Who else might you contact?

In your discussions with attorneys, ask about stories encountered in law school. You will have heard that many public interest jobs are boring or routine with little chance to be creative. Others may have warned you that you lose your chance to ever work in private practice if you take a job in public interest. The preconception that "real" lawyers don't work in the government or nonprofit organizations like hospitals and foundations abounds.

If you have heard these myths or others, ask questions and find out whether the assumptions on which they are based are valid. You will most likely be meeting lawyers who are happy to share their own personal experiences and dispel common myths.

Continue the exploration process by taking a job the summer after your first year that will help you to learn about one of your options and increase your skills. (For more guidance on obtaining summer jobs, contact your placement office or read the chapters on the Job Search which follow and adapt it to the search for summer positions.)

Conclusion

Unfortunately, students graduating from what are considered the most selective law schools display little knowledge of the vast number of lawyers who practice in small firms (i.e., few know that 65% of all lawyers in private practice are in firms of less than six lawyers), have little respect for such practices, and have almost no idea of the range of representation of these lawyers. Even if they are well aware of the overwhelming majority of lawyers who practice in small firms and are interested in joining these practitioners, few students, knowing how little clinical experience they were given in law school, have the confidence it takes to look for positions where they will immediately bear responsibility for representing individuals.

The "Green Man" made an appearance on one episode of the television show *Northern Exposure* constantly advising Ed about his lack of competence and many other reasons why Ed would fail if he pursued the career he envisioned for himself. The Green Man was eventually revealed to be the mythical cause of all evil in the world—the lack of self-esteem.

Law students are introduced to the Green Man early on in their law school years. You will constantly be reminded that there are others who are wiser, more experienced, and more likely to succeed. If you have a vision, however, do not be diverted when the Green Man visits.

Explore your options through relevant courses, knowledgeable faculty or practitioners, part-time or summer jobs, or extracurricular activities to get a clearer picture of what it is like to practice in your chosen area. It may not be easy to make time for a special workshop or set up an interview with an attorney who practices in the field, but keep in mind that you are working on planning a career that genuinely suits your personal and professional goals. Ignore the Green Man and move on to the second year of law school.

7

Analyzing Skills and More Exploring

In the second year of law school, take time to analyze your skills, improve areas which need strengthening, and explore further the areas in which you have an interest. Once again, recognizing that your schedule is a busy one, dividing these tasks up and doing a little bit on a weekly or monthly basis will make them more manageable.

One of the traditional methods used by law schools to place students is on-campus interviewing (OCI.) Despite all the hoopla associated with OCI, law students would be better off ignoring the process altogether. If this seems a little radical, remember Bolles's advice: *do not start with the vacancies.*

OCI and the Problems It Generates

Law students should not start with OCI placement procedures because very few of the legal employers are able to participate in it. Most employers do not know what their hiring needs will be a year in advance and therefore are unprepared to interview the fall students who will graduate the following May or June. The OCI employers tend to be large law firms practicing in a few limited areas of practice, representing as few as 1% of those in the society. As a student, you may begin to believe that the on–campus interviewers are the only credible options when the reality is that they are only a tiny segment of the legal market.

Only a fraction of employers are served by OCI and only a fraction of law students benefit from the process. At some law schools, the large firm presence is limited to visits by nonlawyers who simply screen applicants. These firms seem to be of the opinion that only those who attend "the top" law schools are likely to meet their qualifications.

As the economy weakened in the 90s, fewer law firms interviewed at law schools resulting in fewer students getting jobs through a system that only served a fraction to begin with. Unfortunately, many law schools, rather than viewing this limited presence as an opportunity to provide career information about other options available to graduates, spend an inordinate amount of time and effort trying to prove to these "prestigious" firms how good their students are.

Despite the inherent problems of OCI, many law schools continue to define success in terms of OCI placement. They perpetuate the myth that your placement success can be measured by the amount of dollars you earn the first year out of law school.

Much of this emphasis on OCI stems from the annual *U.S. News and World Report* evaluation of graduate schools which ranks law schools based on a number of factors. One is entitled "Placement Success Rank." This is calculated from a formula which takes into account the percentage of students employed on graduation, the percentage employed six months after graduation, the ratio of the number of graduates to the number of employers recruiting on campus during the year and the average starting salary. Thus the high rating of a law school, in part, depends on getting the most graduates the quickest into the jobs that pay the most; i.e., delivering them up through on-campus interviewing to the largest wealthiest law firms. Unfortunately the *U.S. News and World Report* fails to take into consideration or survey graduates one or two years later to see if they agree they were "successfully" placed.

Many law school faculty and staff members responsible for career services are well aware of these problems. Eighty out of the 100 law school career planners attending a panel indicated support for the elimination of on-campus interviewing. Asked to explain why they could not do so and substitute career planning programs, one cited her dean's focus on the "bottom line"; i.e., jobs at graduation. Over the years others have talked about the desire to increase their schools' prestige or transform it from being viewed as a "regional" school. Devoting time and effort to bringing "prestigious" law firms to the school, the reasoning goes, may lead to more of their students being hired, and eventually increase a school's *U.S. News and World Report* ranking.

As the OCI system continues to guide students to large law firms, it generates a sense of failure for the many graduating students who do not secure one of these positions. The fact is that many of these students would not find a satisfying career in a megafirm or have a chance to practice the type of law that truly interests them. Unfortunately, they are left feeling rejected by a system that they should have avoided in the first place.

Even the students who win the "OCI lottery" may find themselves down the road regretting the fact that they were placed somewhere because someone had an opening. I have heard many stories of lawyers whose most enjoyable legal experience was the position they took in the summer after their first year in law school. On their return to school, however, rather than taking the time to evaluate the positive and negative features of their summer work and analyzing why it was so enjoyable, they were immediately told to draft a resume and decide which of the OCI employers they wanted to interview with. This step was followed in what seemed to be quick and logical succession by a series of interviews, visits to law firms, an offer for the summer, and an offer for permanent employment. Had these same lawyers devoted time to evaluating their previous position in light of how it conformed to their goals instead of someone else's, they may not find themselves among the dissatisfied attorneys years later looking for another type of work.

Learn from these experiences and do not be diverted by the Green Man who questions why anyone would want your skills and talent. The OCI placement method serves few employers, few students, and even fewer students well. Keep in mind that your personal objective is finding a satisfying position and achieving that goal is success as you define it, not someone else.

What'll I Tell my Mom? What'll I Tell my Pa?

You may be thinking, okay, this makes sense to me, but would you explain it to my family and friends?

Actually, I had a student ask me to do just that. A week before graduation, she came to see me and said, "Ron, would you do me a favor? If you see me with my parents at the graduation reception, would you please explain to them that it is acceptable for a Harvard Law School student to graduate without having a job?" She wanted to work on Capitol Hill and knew that to get a position you had to be in D.C. to be able to respond immediately to the notices.

Instead of receiving praise for her law school accomplishments upon graduation, she found herself being judged by the "placement" standard and lost valued family respect, support, and encouragement at a critical time. She moved to D.C. anyway and accepted a position in late December which led to involvement on the national level with a group advocating for issues of significant concern to women.

This young woman took an active role in finding a position that would meet *her* goals, but since she found employment seven months after graduation, she would be counted as a placement failure in the annual *U.S. News and World Report* survey. Like her, you would be wise to ignore OCI, actively plan your career, and choose an opportunity that is best for you. Let's take a closer look at how you might do so.

The Importance of Analyzing Skills

You have now spent a period of time exploring and reading about the options. You have taken courses, joined an organization, read some material and talked to professors and alumni/ae. You took an exploratory job during the year or summer months and have thought about the experience and evaluated it in terms of your goals.

Now you are ready to begin focusing on skills you have or want to have as part of your professional development. In *The Career Planning Guide: From Law Student to Lawyer,* Munneke talks about the importance of analyzing skills in the career choice and job search processes.

> What is right for one person is not necessarily right for someone else. 'What is right' is partially determined by correlating the skills which a job requires and the skills an individual possesses. The closer the match between these two, the greater is the likelihood of finding satisfaction, as well as long-term success, in one's career. (Munneke, *Career Planning Guide*, p. 43, ABA, 1992)

As with the goals analysis, this career planning principle is also discussed in the MacCrate Report. Another fundamental value of the legal profession is not just using your present skills, but developing skills throughout your career. The MacCrate Report confirms that:

> As a member of a learned profession a lawyer should be committed to the value of seeking out and taking advantage of opportunities to increase his or her knowledge and improve his or her skills.

Whether you are seeking your first job as an attorney or your fifth, it is your professional obligation to look for work where you will learn and continually improve the skills you want to use.

What Are Your Skills?

Create a personal inventory by first describing each organization you have worked for (legal and non-legal, paid and volunteer) and the dates you worked there. Then list the skills you used to perform your major responsibilities; i.e., "As head sailing instructor at a camp for 150 boys, I developed an innovative program which included safety and evaluation procedures and supervised and trained a staff of twenty." This will help you to recognize the breadth and depth of your experience and identify your talents and capabilities.

The list of skills on page 50 will serve as a starting point for further skills analysis. It represents a broad cross-section of typical skills used in a variety of disciplines, but is not meant to be comprehensive. You may want to add to the skills listed here or examine similar exercises in career planning books.

First check all the items in the three groups that represent skills that you have or want to have and roles you might see yourself playing in your professional career. Place a "0" next to those that you want to develop but do not believe you have yet gained. After you have finished completing the form, look at what you have selected.

If you find your choices are heavily weighed in Groups A and B, your preference may be the path traditionally taken by lawyers over the last few decades, the use of your legal training in an adversarial setting. You are likely to find the position that is right for you in a private firm or public law firm.

What are the skills you need to prepare yourself and how can you learn them?

The MacCrate Report lists ten fundamental skills of the legal profession which you need to be able to competently represent a client. They include problem solving, factual investigation, communication, counseling, negotiation, managing legal work effectively, and resolving ethical dilemmas. The MacCrate Report recommends that the description of each course in law school catalogues include which fundamental skills and values will be taught and that all summer employment listings state the skills and values that will be learned while carrying out the duties and responsibilities of the position. If this information is not readily available, you should contact members of the faculty and the registrar's office so you can take courses and summer positions that will help you gain and improve these skills.

Clinical courses are often the one place where it is clear which skills are being taught. Unfortunately, there may be no such courses or too few seats available since this teaching approach is not held in high esteem by law schools.

Analyzing Skills and Possible Professional Roles

Step 1: Check all the items within the three groups which represent skills you have or would like to have or professional roles you might play. Place a "0" next to those which you would like to develop but do not yet feel you have.

Step 2: Take a look at your selections and keep the list where you can refer to it when evaluating career options.

Group A	Group B	Group C
___ legal analysis and reasoning	___ initiator	___ creative or artistic skills or imagination
___ consultant	___ priority setter	___ community organizer
___ leader/motivator	___ actor/public speaker	___ teacher, trainer, or educator
___ debater/argument presenter	___ problem solver	___ good listener
___ persuading or influencing others	___ conceptualizing solutions	___ group facilitator or consensus builder
___ investigating facts	___ recognizing or resolving ethical dilemmas	___ team player
___ sales/marketing	___ computer literate	___ program developer or implementer
___ doing legal research and writing	___ financial analysis	___ mediator or conflict resolver
___ drafting commercial documents	___ writing skills	___ policy-maker
___ negotiator	___ oral communication or interviewing	___ general researcher
___ working independently	___ strategic planner	___ creative writing
___ adversarial skills	___ promotor or entrepreneur	___ friendly and caring or person
___ competitor		___ counselor, coach, mentor
___ following litigation procedures		___ networker
___ decision maker		___ people manager
___ arbitrator		
___ organizer or manager of legal team		

In *The High Citadel* by Joel Seligman, the author looks at the one hundred year period since Christopher Langdell, a Harvard Law School dean, conceived the "case method" for the teaching of law students and then had incredible success in convincing most law schools to adopt as their role teaching students simply how to study the law and to think like a lawyer. As a result, the belief that law schools should prepare students to practice law, held by Brandeis among others, was ignored.

At present, therefore, few law students have been exposed to the full range of professional skills offerings, according to the MacCrate Report. The Task Force found that most law students upon graduation had "four or fewer skills 'experiences' (simulated skills, clinics, externships, or others) while in law school" and,

> When classes of first year 'Introduction to Lawyering'...legal writing and research...trial advocacy...and moot court were removed from the list, the majority of graduating students had only one...or no...additional exposures to professional skills instruction....[P]rofessional skills training occupies only nine (9%) percent of the total instructional time available to law schools. (MacCrate, p. 240)

If one compares the way law schools teach law to the way medical schools teach medicine, the problems inherent in law schools becomes even more apparent. Consider a revision of the medical school curriculum. Instead of going into the hospitals, the clinics, and the laboratories, instead of working on cadavers and treating patients, the four years would be spent in large classes with faculty members who, after two years of reviewing grants at the National Institute of Health, started teaching medical students how to think like a doctor.

Clearly, as the MacCrate Report puts it, "Much remains to be done to improve the preparation of new lawyers for practice."

One of its recommendations, MRR 2, has been formally adopted by the House of Delegates of the American Bar Association. Standard 301 (a) (one of the guidelines for law school accreditation) regarding a law school's educational program has been amended by clarifying its reference to qualifying "graduates for admission to the bar" by adding: "and to prepare them to participate effectively in the legal profession." MRR 2 also includes the following: "This would affirm that education in lawyering skills and professional values is central to the mission of law schools and recognize the current stature of skills and values instruction."

There is general agreement that if you plan to work in a small firm, there will likely not be the time to give you close supervision.

While the advantage is that you gain the training that comes with assuming responsibility, it is also important that you have many of the skills needed and are able to "hit the ground running."

"[S]tudents who expect to enter practice in a relatively unsupervised practice setting have a special need for opportunities to obtain skills instruction," as the MacCrate Report points out. If the skills training offered at your school is inadequate, you should consider other options outside the traditional curriculum, such as taking a paid or volunteer position during the school year or summer months.

Some argue against work during the academic year because students need to concentrate on studies in order to get good grades and a job. Munneke refers to this dilemma when he states, "Choices about how to balance your education and work experience inevitably must be made in light of the career planning process. In other words, what you should do now depends on where you want to go later."

While your classload during the year may be too heavy to have a full-time or hectic job on the side, consider all your options before buying into the concept that you don't have time for anything else. Outside work may impair your grade-point average, but to what degree? Many competent, satisfied lawyers believe law school teaching methods are generally not educationally sound and that they learned very little in law school that is useful in their practice. Find out how much of a factor grades are for successful job candidates in the field and type of position you desire. Many public interest and small firm employers ignore grades when considering applicants for an opening relying more on commitment and experience. If you want to gain skills and explore your fields of interest then working while still in law school may be your top priority.

Volunteer Experiences

You might also consider joining with other students to create an extra-curricular organization to assist others. This is the route that has been taken by numerous students on behalf of battered women or other causes they feel strongly about.

While this would be a different experience from working at a firm and should not replace a course given by a practicing attorney, it is very worthwhile to participate to gain hands-on experience as well as knowledge of the area and the issues faced by your clients.

The ABA Law Student Division encourages public service and

professional development projects among individual law schools by providing both how-to pamphlets and seed money to schools seeking to begin programs. Your law school may already sponsor a Work-A-Day program or other special events to promote volunteerism among law students. If not, contact the Law Student Division at (312) 988-5624 for pamphlets on how to initiate a project to tutor students, help renovate houses, or other worthwhile projects.

Choosing Another Direction: Advocacy

If your preferences on the skills analysis exercise fall primarily within Groups B and C, your ideal position may be with a nonprofit organization. Informal surveys of clients and workshop participants indicate that as high as 33% of all law students and lawyers fit into this category.

They want to help the sick, the aged, or the poor, but make it clear that they do not want to go to court, do not to want to spend their days taking depositions, reading cases, doing research on motions, preparing briefs, or arguing with other lawyers. They realize that they do not want to use their legal training or practice law in the narrow traditional path. Perhaps you prefer to pursue justice using many of the creative skills you possess combined with your experience in social work, education, or the arts.

Before you decide that being a litigator is not for you, however, take some time to reflect on why you feel this way. Extraordinary results have been achieved by lawyers working through the courts and many attorneys derive incredible satisfaction from such efforts. Ask yourself if your reluctance is based on a feeling that you are not competent to undertake such a complex form of practice. You may think you are not good enough to be a trial lawyer when all you are lacking is experience, education, and preparation. You have so much to contribute to society and there are thousands of organizations in dire need of someone with your talents.

Since law schools often fail to teach the skills needed to represent a client in court, many law students or law school graduates share a feeling of incompetence and lack of self-confidence. I believe the rampant lack of self-esteem is approaching epidemic proportions among lawyers and law students as a result. The Green Man has been able to find full-time employment in the legal profession.

If you have not had any litigation experience, participate in the process in court or before an administrative body, even if your experience is limited to volunteering to assist a litigator for three weeks during your winter recess. Work with those who represent causes you are in sympathy with to test your skills, your interest, and your assumptions. Then re-evaluate your decision not to pursue litigation as an option. As you analyze the skills you have and improve those you need to reach your goals, your self-confidence will rise.

Many of the fundamental lawyering skills are used by those working for nonprofit organizations, especially those in counsel positions, and the comments above about taking clinical courses and working during the academic year are equally applicable. If you need to acquire additional skills with a view towards involvement in policy-making and management, you will probably have to look outside the law school for guidance on developing them. Many who have an interest in these aspects of advocacy came to law school with those skills.

One of the weaknesses of law school training is that the learning of advocacy skills is accomplished through the use of cases, reading how others craft their arguments, and the implication that a "real lawyer" is one who uses his or her legal training in court. My discussions with students over the last number of years indicate there is a great interest in working on legislative efforts, but law schools fail to encourage a career path involving lawmaking. I have always found it ironic when conventional law school wisdom implies that those who work for an organization like Common Cause, drafting and lobbying for the enactment of laws, are not seen as being "real" lawyers. While the value of litigation is often exalted, the art of advocacy, outside the courtroom or within a negotiation session, is too often ignored. An alternative view of advocacy is to see its important role within a democracy, as Jeremy Rifkin maintains in writing about the United States Bicentennial:

> The believers in democracy advocated freedom of expression and the right to self-determination; cooperative enterprise; government of the people, by the people, for the people; conscience above property and institutions. They maintained an interest in the new, the untried, the unexplored; they kept confidence in the ability of the people to create a more just and humane world.

Even those who spend their day advocating on behalf of the underprivileged or underrepresented, may fail to see their work as practicing law. A former Commissioner of Social Services for New York City, in a talk to law students at his alma mater, Fordham Law School, described his successful efforts to close welfare hotels, create summer camps for disadvantaged young, and fight for regulations that would improve the lives of the urban poor. In his twenty minute talk, however, he mentioned three times that he was not practicing law or words to that effect. What a tragedy that he and so many others like him whose work is in the finest tradition of advocacy should believe that they are not in the mainstream simply because they did not pursue the narrow litigation path.

If you decide upon the non-litigation approach, be aware of the pressures and subtle influences that you will encounter. Try to remember, when your classmates talk about the firms they will be working for, that you have a plan as to how you would use your legal training and it may not include practicing law in the traditional sense. Be prepared for their comments when you discuss your plan because they will very likely tell you that "real lawyers do not go to work as in-house counsel for a pro-choice organization" or that "nonprofit work is for losers who can't make it in the firms." When friends and family warn you not to "waste your law school degree," tell them you have no intention of wasting either your degree or your life.

According to W. Chesterfield Smith, former president of the American Bar Association, the true role of lawyers is counselor and healer, the caring non-adversarial and mediator. The time is long overdue for the definition of the practice of law to be broadened by those within the legal profession and the respect given to the "counsellor" role in the phrase "counsellor at law."

Conclusion

Continue to explore the possibilities, increase your skills, and take relevant courses, keeping your goals and values constantly in mind. Get involved in extracurricular activities and take a position during the summer between second and third years that will increase your skills and help you learn about your options.

8
Evaluating the Market and Narrowing Your Options

Immediately upon your return to law school for your third year, evaluate your summer experience, using the Characteristics and Goals in Your Ideal Workplace exercise on page 32.

Being practical, we know that the reason most of the public is not represented is because they can not afford to pay for the legal services they need. Unfortunately, this leads to the assumption too often made by law students and lawyers that there are only a limited number of public interest job openings for those who graduate.

The reality is that there are unlimited number of paid opportunities for graduating law students to use their legal education to help people with the problems they face in their daily lives in the areas of health, housing, education, employment, civil rights, family, and the environment. Let's assume that the 40% of first year law students who express an interest in "doing something that matters" with their degree still feel that way when they graduate three years later and are ready to look for their first legal position. Here's how those 14,000 (40% of the total number of law school students graduating annually) can begin their careers in public interest law.

In the traditional public interest areas, there are about 2,400 legal services offices and about 1,600 public defender offices listed in the National Legal Aid and Defender Association (NLADA) directory; and about 1,000 traditional public interest litigating organizations. That's a total of about 5,000 offices, not lawyers. Assuming that each office hires just one attorney every four years, that would amount to 1,250 annual openings for graduates. (In reality, the number of openings may be much higher as the Legal Aid Society of New York may hire 125 attorneys yearly for its Criminal Defense Division alone.)

Now let's move from possible openings in the public law firm category to the world of private law firms. Remember that there are 550,000 lawyers in private practice in 296,000 firms and that two-thirds of all lawyers in private practice are in firms with five or less lawyers.

These firms include many begun by lawyers formerly in government and legal services who have gone into private practice to represent only individuals and consumers in areas like civil rights, housing, and consumer law. They also include thousands started by lawyers whose practices are limited to the representation of families, women and children, those injured by the dumping of toxic waste, and other underrepresented groups. These firms hire attorneys who share their interests, perhaps not every year, but they do hire. Let's assume that there are, on the average, only 500 such offices in each state and that they only hire recent graduates every fourth year. That's another 6,250 openings yearly.

Now add in openings for graduates who want to use their legal skills in advocacy in non-law firm settings. There are 900,000 non-profits who have obtained federal tax exempt status and thousands of other organizations which fall into this nonprofit category. Assuming there are, on average, only 500 in each state that will have appropriate openings and only one opening every four years, they would generate another 6,250 openings each year nationally.

This leaves 250 graduates who still need a job. Many of them if given support and encouragement would start their own institutions or firms. We know there is the need. They would have more than enough work to keep their new institutions busy.

Law students are rarely encouraged to start a new firm or found an institution. Of the more than 2,500 able, creative students who graduated from Harvard Law School during the years 1984–1989 while I was on staff there, I counted only four graduates who left to start their own business, practice, or institution. Two started "City Year," the role model for President Clinton's national service program. Two others went to San Antonio to start a legal services program. Despite their successes, I find it discouraging that such a small fraction, four out of 2,500 or less than one quarter of one percent, had the self-confidence and the initiative to venture out on their own.

Why do law schools fail to encourage students to start their own practice? Perhaps it is the Socratic method of teaching which fosters conformity and a respect for authority or the fact that the law student's main role models in school are faculty, most of whom are not solo practitioners, but full-time employees. At any rate, there is a constant focus on being an employee which discourages entrepreneurship, risk taking, creativity, autonomy, or the taking of responsibility.

In reality, there is no mystery to beginning an institution or a practice. You, with others, may perhaps have started an organization in high school, college, or law school, and know the rewards of finding a need and filling it. There are an estimated 240,000,000 members of the public unserved by the legal profession! Why not create something which serves them, such as a public interest law center, a private law firm that limits itself to serving those underserved by the traditional bar, a group legal services program, or a consulting firm based on providing knowledge or skills in a special field that interests you, such as environmental law?

For ten years after graduating from law school, Dan Burnstein represented individuals in personal injury cases and incorporated and advised numerous nonprofit organizations. For five years he produced interactive video disks which allowed law students to learn substantive and procedural law and he is now developing software for lawyers and business people to help them improve their negotiation skills. Burnstein has also been active for the past twelve years as a founder, board member, and current president of the Center for Atomic Radiation Studies (CARS), the only organization dedicated to understanding the benefits and dangers associated with the human health effects of radiation.

The focus of CARS is on atomic veterans, victims of human experimentation, and populations located near nuclear power plants. According to Burnstein, CARS is responsible for discovering the Fernald School "Science Club" experiment. It is his work with CARS that has satisfied some of his deepest goals despite his many accomplishments as a lawyer and software developer.

"My legal training has helped me keep focused on the task of social change and education," Burnstein explains. "When questions arise such as, 'Do we have the right to do this?' it is very helpful to have the answer."

Burnstein believes knowledge of the law helps prevent his organization from getting bogged down in legal questions which others may spend an inordinate amount of time on.

"You can keep the nonprofit organization focused on its mission by stripping away what might otherwise be distracting legal non-issues."

As founder of CARS, Burnstein has built a team consisting of the organization's board of directors and staff to work for a common cause. He likes the intellectual stimulation derived from analyzing issues and developing the educational materials and programs for CARS that no one else is providing. Most of all, he says, he enjoys being involved "in a matter that is of vital concern to many people whose cause I believe in and helping to bring about social change through our organization."

Lawyers have a long tradition of being independent and autonomous. That is one of the benefits of being a professional person. Half the lawyers in private practice are *sole* practitioners. None of them found their jobs through an ad. They created their own businesses.

Similarly, many lawyers have chosen to begin an institution when they found an overwhelming need for a particular legal service. There would have been no NAPIL without Mike Caudell-Feagan, no Ayuda without Leslye Orloff. Doug Ladson founded the Legal Action Center for the Homeless. Ralph Nader and others he brought in have been responsible for establishing many public interest agencies. The National Organization of Women, the Juvenile Law Center, the Center for Constitutional Rights, and the National Wildlife Federation were all started by individuals who saw a need and wanted to fill it. There is an urgent public need for legal services.

If this option appeals to you, but you are not sure of your ability to start an institution or practice, take courses or work in jobs where you will learn how to manage cases and operate a business. Create a place to serve a need.

What about the Money?

What do these positions in public interest law pay? Can you afford to practice in this area?

Law school is expensive. Some economists in the 80s could "prove" that a law school education was a good investment if the graduate took a high paying job in a large law firm to pay off loans and still have a reasonable amount of disposable income left over. As a result, the myth that pervades the law schools arose that one could not "afford" anything other than these positions.

One obvious solution is to reduce the amount you borrow. Calculate the minimum you need and borrow only that amount. Don't fall into the trap of assuming that you need to borrow as much as the school is willing to give you. You may not need that much to live on.

Another way to reduce the amount you borrow is to earn income through term-time employment. As discussed earlier, while some law schools discourage this, especially in the first year, working provides two benefits. It reduces your debt and provides legal training and experience the law school usually does not offer. As noted earlier, while some argue that part-time employment during law school will hurt your grades, the firms that use grades as the sole determining factor in hiring may not be places you would find satisfaction.

Another possibility is working full time and having that employer contribute towards your law school education. It's true that it will take longer to get through law school, but thousands of attorneys have done it, including many who were working for an organization they believed in and were encouraged by the organization to pursue a legal education and continue their career there in another, higher ranking position.

Since the approach outlined in this book assumes that the position you find will not have been advertised and will have had few "applicants," more consideration will be given to the person and his or her experience and proven commitment to an area rather than grades.

Do not make the assumption that you cannot afford to work in an area without knowing the salary range for the opportunities you are seeking. A cursory glance at the publicized job notices reveals that for a variety of the positions described here the salaries range from $28,000 to $35,000. Estimate your monthly income, taxes, loan payments, and expenses upon graduation. The result is an approximation of your monthly surplus or deficit. Keep in mind that this figure is only true for the first year of practice and does not take into account salary increases.

First and second year students should use the same sort of financial analysis when considering summer employment rather than assuming they must take a job, any job, which earns as much as possible over the summer months. If you go along with the "I can't afford to do it" myth, you might forfeit an opportunity during the first and second summers to try a new experience which may help you plan your career. There are summer jobs in the public interest field available with salary ranges of $250 to $500 a week.

In addition, there are other alternatives for summer employment. You might be able to obtain a grant to subsidize working in public interest from a NAPIL-connected, student-funded fellowship, a public interest organization, the federal government through work study, or one of the few law school-funded programs.

You should also check to see if your school has a loan forgiveness program. A number of schools have made an effort to lessen the profound effect of high debt by reducing or forgiving some portion of the loans for some graduates taking full time public interest law positions. A word of caution, however, as they may be inapplicable to graduates who go to work for private law firms or nonprofit organizations.

Balancing Priorities

A most critical issue is how much weight you should give to income. First, realize that income is relative based on several factors. The high paying salaries of major law firms may make the news, but it costs a lot more to live in the urban areas where they are located than in the small town or medium-sized city where you may choose to practice. Also, some of that income must go towards keeping up a certain image in terms of the type of clothes you wear, clubs or groups you belong to, and even the type of car you drive.

Taking all this into consideration, you may find that your ideal job is still not going to pay the kind of salary offered, say for instance, your classmate who goes to work for a large corporation. Stop and think, though, what the potential negative consequences are of pursuing a job based on financial reward as your primary factor. What value do you place on the many factors that play a role in job satisfaction? *How much are you willing to give up to earn a lot of money?*

Matthew P. Dumont, a psychiatrist who worked for community mental health centers, points out that identifying who is wealthy and who is poor can not always be defined by income alone.

> But what is poverty? It soon became evident to me that what is pathogenic about it is not merely the lack of money. The amount of money, the buying power, commanded by a welfare recipient in Chelsea [Massachusetts] would have been like a king's ransom to any member of a thriving hunter-gatherer tribe in the Kalahari. Yet the life of the welfare recipient appears terribly impoverished in contrast to that of the tribe member. A closer observation of life in Chelsea resolves the paradox. Chelsea residents possess material things unknown to the hunter but, despite this [meager] purchasing power, they experience little control over the circumstances of their existence....The earliest discriminator of social class is the relative sense of control over the events in one's life....Lower class children learn tragi-

cally early that things happen to them, that they are acted upon by life rather than being the operative agents in its history....**Powerlessness in the face of life events seems to be the final common path of urban poverty....The more one is exposed to events over which one has no control, the more one is convinced that there is no control over anything.** (Matthew P. Dumont, "An Unfolding– Memoir of Community Mental Health," *Readings: A Journal of Reviews and Commentary in Mental Health,* September, 1989.)

It is ironic that many lawyers who have successfully pursued the high income offered by the large law firms now find themselves with a wealth of material goods but living, in a way, in abject poverty because they do not feel they have control over their lives. Try to imagine what it must be like for the partner in the large New York law firm who talks about having no self respect, no self-confidence, no self-esteem, no direct contact with individuals, no belief that she was contributing to the public good, no intellectual stimulation, and no autonomy.

Contrast her view of her life with that of a public interest attorney who gives this analysis of income:

Here's how I view my salary in comparison with the salaries of my classmates in the private sector. I am 'spending' not receiving $50,000 a year for a job I love. I feel good about what I've done when I go home each night. That's disposable 'income' well spent.

The hours that come with a high income often mean giving up other things, including freedom to spend your evenings and weekends as you see fit. There are lawyers who will tell you they have never been to Parents' Night at their child's school or seen one of their child's ball games. As one parent put it:

Operating my own law firm allows me greater latitude than a 'big firm' would in the balancing act required in the mixing of a full time law practice and the nurturing of a family.

Having time to enjoy your family and friends, your hobbies and volunteer interests is an important part of living well. Even if you are a single now and willing to work a 60-hour week, the day may come when you resent it.

What is the value of your professional degree? "To the student, the value of a professional degree often is determined by its worth on the job market," according to *U.S. News and World Report* (March 19, 1990 issue.)

Perhaps that is true for some, but most of you reading this guide believe that your law degree is important because it increases your likelihood of finding satisfaction in your work and the sense of self-worth that accompanies it. You know that it increases the possibility of your contributing to the common good by involving you in matters of great importance to the society. You value autonomy and the ability to participate in decisions that affect your life. You want to use both your mind and your talents to the fullest capacity. Your degree should enable you to experience all of these characteristics which add up to a full professional life.

Narrowing Your Options

At the end of the fall of your third year, it is time to analyze what you have learned and make some decisions. Take time to rank your priorities and narrow your options.

A common quote heard among graduating law students is "I want to keep my options open." This sounds good, but it actually is a terrible career planning guideline. Even those who keep their options open will eventually end up working somewhere. The difference is that they will usually be selected by someone else rather than choosing what they want to do. Keeping your options open should result in a random placement with as much likelihood of career satisfaction as having the Publishers Clearing House's Mobile Van arrive at your apartment telling you have won $20,000,000.

Having said this, I caution you not to be so narrowly focused that your job search is doomed from the start. If there are few opportunities in a field and none of them pay enough for you to be able to afford reasonable expenses, your search is bound to be frustrating.

You should insure that your option is a realistic one, but there are thousands of opportunities for you in careers serving the legal needs of the public. In order to find one that suits you and your goals, you must be committed to making the decisions. You decide:

- what your personal and professional goals are;
- what skills you want to use;
- where you want to live;
- what practice setting you prefer;
- who you want to represent; and
- what substantive areas appeal to you.

You have had a number of work experiences, taken courses, been involved in extracurricular activities, attended panels, read accounts, talked to lawyers. You know what you like. The exercise on pages 64–65 will help you write it down.

Clarifying Options

Fill in the blanks below and on the following page to help you articulate what your ideal job might be and narrow your options.

1. I want to live and work in this geographic area:

2. I want to work in this setting:

Public Law Firm

Legal Services
Public Interest Litigation Organization
Public Defender

Private Law Firm

Non-Profit Organization

3. The salary range is:

4. Such a position satisfies the following personal and professional goals: *(See Chapter 3)*

5. It allows me to use, gain and improve these skills: *(Use the list in Chapter 4)*

6. I will be representing the following populations:
___ children
___ women
___ the poor
___ the homeless
___ the sick
___ the disabled
___ minorities
___ immigrants
___ families
___ elderly
___ employees
___ consumers
___ veterans
___ others (specify) _____

7. I will be involved in the following substantive areas:
___ discrimination, civil rights, civil liberties
___ women's rights
___ elderly
___ gay and lesbian rights
___ welfare, poverty, homelessness
___ urban economic development
___ environmental law
___ health law issues, mental health, disability rights
___ employment/labor
___ food and hunger
___ landlord and tenant, housing development
___ criminal law
___ consumer goods and services
___ education
___ immigration, international human rights
___ family law generally, child custody
___ rural life issues
___ military justice/veterans' rights
___ children and youth
___ first amendment/media
___ adoption, guardianship, wills and estates
___ other (specify) _____

Conclusion

In law school the common wisdom is that you can't afford to go into public interest and few do. Since many believe this, few explore the options and even fewer do it, a self-fulfilling prophecy.

Most of the lawyers who come looking for advice on how to make a transition to public interest law spend very little time talking about financial constraints. Income is no longer the prime consideration.

Never accept advice from anyone that begins by suggesting that you trade all your goals for a high salary. Some may even advise you to take a job with a large law firm for a few years to pay off the loans "and then you can find work consistent with your values and beliefs." This is the certain path to personal disillusionment and unhappiness, makes no sense, and is unprofessional.

W. Chesterfield Smith believed that the goal of legal practice is not the accumulation of wealth but the obligation to see that all persons have a lawyer at a reasonable price. Remember the fundamental value that you should select a position that is consistent with *your* goals and allows you to improve your skills.

9
The Search for a Satisfying Position

As the winter of your third year begins you should start the search for your ideal position.

To many of your classmates, this search means submitting a resume to the placement office and waiting for an on-campus interview or mailing the resume to those employers who send job notices to the law school. By now, however, you should realize that such typical placement procedures are not likely to result in your finding the position you want for several reasons.

The first reason is that, as noted above, those law firms that interview consist of a very small segment of the legal profession and only by a random act of coincidence will any one of them be the option consistent with your personal and professional goals and with the skills you want to use. Using OCI and responding to ads constantly pits you against hundreds of qualified people for jobs. If there are, say, 200 resumes submitted for an opening, 190 of them will be eliminated right off the bat. For most job seekers, this leads to much soul-searching about why they were not considered qualified and may lead to a lack of self-confidence or panic that they will not get a job upon graduation.

The second reason traditional placement activities are not likely to help you find a satisfying position is that very few openings are ever advertised in writing. Career planners may differ on the percentages, but all agree that only a small percentage of all openings are going to be read about. Look at a resource such as *Good Works*. (See listing on pp. 74–75.) Included within the description of each organization is information about how it advertises job openings. Note the frequency of the phrase *word-of-mouth*. These openings never appear in writing perhaps due to the lack of staff needed to distribute notices and process hundreds of resumes or the costs involved in advertising.

Thirdly, it cannot be overemphasized that most jobs in any field are publicized when the position is available, not months or years ahead of time. Traditional placement activities automatically limit the search to the few employers who can predict what their needs will be nine or ten months down the road. Few employers operate that way.

Keep this in mind: Only a small percentage of the positions you want are advertised in writing or interviewed for at the law schools. Most open up at the same time the employer wants the individual to begin working. In other words, *the most satisfying position for you may not be advertised until after you graduate or it may not be advertised at all.*

Once you understand this, you must realize that you need to learn an approach which will help you, both before and after graduation, to find these openings that few are aware of. Remember Munneke's advice that career planning must precede the search process: you have to know what you are looking for if you expect to find it.

Since your primary objective is workplace satisfaction, you have already identified your personal and professional goals, taken note of your skills and which skills you still need to develop, and used summertime or part-time work experiences as a way to find out more about a particular field. By ranking your priorities, you have a good idea of what type of law interests you, the employment setting you think you would enjoy, where you would like to work, the salary range you are willing to accept, and so forth.

You know from your research that there are many opportunities for you in your chosen field. With the conviction that comes from knowing you truly want the work you are seeking, you can focus your intellect and your energy on the challenge it presents. Now you are ready to begin the job search phase.

Munneke breaks the job search into five steps: packaging yourself, researching potential employers, building a network, selling yourself, and making a decision. Let's take a closer look at each of these steps within the context of finding a legal position which serves the needs of the public.

Packaging Yourself

Consider yourself and the services which you can provide as a product which you are going to try to sell in the marketplace. You want to present yourself in such a way that best allows potential employers to recognize that you are the most qualified person for the position.

This can be accomplished in several ways. Suppose you have already determined that you would like to work in a small firm that does immigration law. You have taken immigration law courses and sat in on a half-day seminar offered by the county bar association. During your second year of law school, you served as a volunteer for a student international human rights group and worked part-time for the National Immigration Project. By analyzing your skills, you know that you are a good listener, a problem-solver, a counselor, and a caring person. You have kept up your ability to speak Spanish fluently by tutoring an elementary student three times a week. To support yourself as an undergrad, you started a house painting service one summer and you know the experience of running your own business will prove valuable. Based on your notes from courses taken, the bar association seminar, and reading articles about the field, you know two or three firms that specialize in immigration law, some of the lawyers' names who practice in this area, and what the newest developments are. As a result, you can present yourself as someone with the desired qualifications, credentials, and commitment needed to secure a position in your chosen area of interest. You will, of course, want to include these skills and experiences when compiling your resume.

But merely putting them together as a resume alone and mass mailing it will not be enough to land a position no matter how good your resume is. There are, as Bolles notes in *What Color Is your Parachute?*, thousands of resumes sent every day which never result in a job. He estimates that "only one job offer is tendered and accepted in the whole world of work, for every 1,470 resumes that are floating around out there."

Bolles cites a six-year survey by an outplacement firm which showed that 68% of its candidates found their jobs through personal contacts, 15% through a search firm's activities, 9% by answering classified ads, and only 8% by doing a mass mailing of their resumes or a letter.

My conversations with job-hunters, over the years, have convinced me that there is a passionate belief in resumes that is out of all proportion to how often they in fact ever get anyone an interview for a job. I think the faith placed in resumes is a very misplaced faith. For every person you know who did get a job-interview by sending out resumes, I know ninety-nine who didn't. *(What Color Is your Parachute?)*

Bolles believes that there is actual harm in sending out resumes. "Job-hunters who invest a lot of time on sending out their resume, often suffer tremendous damage to their self-esteem when their resumes are rejected or ignored."

He suggests the resume be used as a "memory jogger" to be left with the employer after the interview. He refers to an old career-counseling principle: A resume is something you should never send ahead of you, but always leave behind you.

Accepting Bolles's view that the resume is not the be-all, end-all way of getting a job, you still need to put together something to be left behind. Having gone through the process of exploring your goals, skills, and options and having selected your preference, now is the time to prepare a resume because now you know who you are looking to work with and why you are qualified.

Look again at your personal inventory and your other notes. Can you identify specific things you have done that relate to positions in your particular area? For example, an elder law firm would care that 30% per cent of the clients in your poverty law clinic were elderly, and that you know the issues, terminology, and regulations.

If you want to concentrate on landlord/tenant issues, can you demonstrate you have the necessary skills for this type of practice, even though you may never have worked on a landlord/tenant case per se? Perhaps you have never appeared before the rent control board, but you may have gone through a similar process for a hearing with another board while still in school.

If you desire to be an advocate, plan to stress your experience writing, advising, teaching, lobbying, and other related skills. A law student who clerked for a firm involved in a big case or a young lawyer who has already demonstrated court skills may have impressive litigation skills or experiences, but if you know you do not want to spend your life as a litigator, do not elaborate on them in the resume.

As a quick exercise, look at the most recent version of your resume. Based on what you have learned about yourself and what your highest priority is, can you think of two items which you now know should be expanded and highlighted in your resume? Are there volunteer experiences, college activities, or skills which should have been included? Create a resume which demonstrates how qualified you are for the field of your choice.

Note that this approach is different from the currently popular idea that a resume should be a generic or "one page fits all" document which can be altered, resulting in a different version for every type of employer or opening. This sounds good, but is not really an effective way to package yourself. Consider the difficulty of developing an effective plan to market an undefined product to the entire range of customers. Suppose, for example, an auto manufacturer tried to develop a vehicle that could serve as a mini-van, a sports car, a luxury sedan, a pick-up truck, and a tractor all in one and tried to sell it to every American.

Another version of trying to please everyone is the current practice of eliminating all references to involvement in social issues (gay rights, abused women, the sick, or the poor) because it might hurt your chances of being hired. The implication by students and lawyers who do this is that they might become a partner if they don't express their values and beliefs for seven years, a sure-fire route to dissatisfaction.

Instead of trying to please everybody, build your resume on your strengths, skills, and professional goals. Such a resume is likely to be looked at seriously by those who have an opening in your area or kept by those who might have an opening in the future. It might also be forwarded to another employer or organization looking for someone with commitment, competence, and experience in their area.

Researching Potential Employers or Possible Contacts

Now that you know who you are and what you have to offer, or to state it in marketing terms, what your product is, you need to develop a list of potential workplaces or target population. Since you have already decided the geographic region in which you want to work, your search will be more focused, more efficient, more productive, and more likely to result in finding a satisfying opportunity.

Chapter 8 offered a preview into potential employers, but now you should be able to do more thorough research leading to possible openings. Having narrowed your field and done some coursework and reading, you will know what resources you need to obtain and what you are looking for in them.

You will soon discover that friends or acquaintances may become resources once you know where you are heading. Take a look at the resources listed on page 74 to uncover sources available to you.

Let's use an example to show how you can take advantage of all of these references in your job search. Suppose you want to practice in the area of family law with a focus on the problems of women and children in a traditional setting; i.e., a group legal practice concentrating on both litigation and mediation.

Staff at the CSO or your Alumni/ae Office should have the list of alumni/ae in those fields in hardcopy but you might also use on-line computer services referred to previously to locate them as well as to develop verified mailing lists of individual and organizational contacts; i.e., Lexis' Martindale-Hubbell, Public Interest Employer Directory and its National Directory of Legal Aid and Defenders Offices (names, addresses, and telephone numbers of the civil Legal Services Programs, Public Defender offices, State-wide associations of criminal defense lawyers, programs for special needs and support services programs; Westlaw's NALP Directory of Legal Employers Database (mostly large firms), legal periodicals and newspapers, and its Practice Areas; and the vast resources available to you on Prodigy, America On-Line, CompuServe and the Internet. You can develop mailing lists, identify contacts and verify addresses on-line either at the law school or, with proper software, from your home computer.

The section on public law firms refers you to resources that list juvenile law centers and legal services programs where issues include not only spousal abuse, but also housing, benefits, and education. Under private law firms, you will find your law school's listing of small firm family law practices, national, state, and local bar associations and minority or women's bar associations which all may have their own family law section, specialty bar associations, such as the American Academy of Matrimonial Lawyers or the Academy of Family Mediators, juvenile law committees of these associations, family court dockets, and family service officers.

A directory of associations at your local library will list nonprofit organizations serving juveniles and women which may be able to provide you with the names of those who provide them with legal assistance.

Your own circle of family and friends is easily expanded to include friends of your parents, your spouse's family, your co-workers' friends, a friend of a friend from college days, and so forth. Many of these acquaintances will know someone who practices family law or juvenile law, have been involved in a case themselves or know someone who has, have a cousin who works for a lawyer as a paralegal, etc.

As you continue to enlist the help of friends, family, other students, law school faculty and staff, alumni, and practicing lawyers you will be amazed at how much easier it is for them to lead you to other resources if, rather than saying, "Can you help me find work serving the legal needs of the public somewhere in the country?" you ask "I want to help victims of spousal abuse in Cincinnati. Who represents them?"

All of these resources may lead to potential employers or further information—a book, an article, a video, or an organization—which can help you locate them. Remember: most jobs are obtained via personal contacts.

Suppose you would like to work with a nonprofit organization on environmental issues. The significant difference here is that you are more likely to find your target employers at a graduate school of public health, or in the office of the sponsor of Earth Day, at the public library, or at a bookstore than at a law school where the emphasis is on law firms. Do not, however, ignore some of those listed. Ask faculty to refer you to, and look at the alumni/ae records for, lawyers who work for nonprofits. Look at *Good Works* and *Public Interest Profiles. The Law and Business Directory of Corporate Counsel, Volume 2* lists many lawyers who work for nonprofits and has a section where all lawyers are listed by law school attended (for ease, I assume, in using the "old person network.") Your undergraduate school may also be a helpful source of materials and referrals.

These are just a few resources I have found useful, and the list is in no way intended to be all-inclusive. Once you recognize that the goal is to find those who are doing what you want to do, you will quickly discover other resources. Although the search for your chosen area, be it juvenile law, the environment, or criminal law field, or any advocacy area such as education or health, will ultimately lead to different resources, the approach will be the same.

Building a Network

The list of resources shows how family, friends, and acquaintances can contribute to your efforts to build a network of contacts. Now that you have focused on the type of position you are seeking, you will be able to provide clear guidance to those who want to help you. But setting your goals, writing a resume, and having many acquaintances is not going to automatically lead to a job unless you are extremely lucky. *You must take positive action to ensure that those in your field of choice who need help find out about your availability.*

Resources in the Search for Contacts or Potential Employers

Within Law Schools

Law school faculty and staff
Law student evaluations of summer positions
Directories of alumni/ae and their areas of practice
Alumni/ae work accounts (i.e., Harvard's *Alumni/ae in Action Part II* 1994, or *Yale Law Graduates at Work*)
Alumni/ae mentors
Panels of practicing lawyers
Job listings (permanent and part-time)
Law School Public Interest Law Support Programs: A Directory (Lists a range of public interest programs available to law students, such as fellowships and summer internships, student organizations, law journals, mandatory pro bono requirements, voluntary pro bono opportunities, specialized career services, and clinical programs. For further information or to purchase a copy, write Elissa C. Lichtenstein, Public Service Division, American Bar Association, 740 15th Street NW, Ninth Floor, Washington, DC 20005)

Public Law Firms

NAPIL Guide to Public Interest Legal Internships (annual)
NAPIL Guide to Post-Graduate Fellowships (annual)
Directory of Public Interest Law Centers published by the Alliance for Justice
City directories of public interest organizations (i.e., *Washington Council of Lawyers Directory*)
Job Market Previews, National Clearinghouse for Legal Services, Inc.
Directory of Legal Aid and Defender Offices

Private Law Firms

Listings compiled by law schools of small law firms
National Lawyers Guild National Referral Directory
National and Federal Legal Employment Report
Bar association committees
Continuing legal education course faculty lists
Local courts, referrals from court personnel and case dockets with names of attorneys

Lists of members of relevant organizations (i.e., *National Association of Criminal Defense Lawyers, American Immigration Lawyers Association, Trial Lawyers for Public Justice*)
Martindale Hubbell

Nonprofit Organizations

National Directory of Nonprofit Organizations
Good Works (4th Edition 1993/1994) Barricade Books, Inc.
Public Interest Profiles, Foundation for Public Affairs
Law and Business Directory of Corporate Counsel, Volume 2
The Road Not Taken, National Association for Law Placement
Community Jobs, Access: Networking in the Public Interest
Undergraduate school faculty, staff and alumni

Others

Drawing from family members, friends, and others, consider contacting those who are attorneys themselves or who work with attorneys, those who have neighbors or acquaintances who practice in your chosen field, and those who have hired attorneys to help them with a legal matter.
Other students from law school, undergraduate school, or high school
Present or former employers and co-workers

Research continues by keeping up with new developments via professional journals and other legal publications. Many will include advertisements for openings and while you know by now that very few appropriate positions are found by responding to an ad, read through them, even outdated ones, to familiarize yourself with the job descriptions, skills required, and agencies who hire. Periodicals will also provide you with the names of those who work in this field and those who write about new developments. Of course, a small percentage of graduating students do find jobs through ads. It also serves to remind you that organizations which do what you want to do, do hire.

From your informational interviewing, your personal inventory, and your research you have compiled a list of many individuals and organizations, numerous places where you might like to work. Unfortunately, however, you do not know of any openings.

What you have to do next has been described in many ways, including *networking* and *self-advocacy*. Continuing the marketing analogy, it might be called *promotion*. Whatever term is used, the reality is that you have to work with and through people and make them aware of your skills, competence, and commitment.

Keep in mind the difference between marketing and sales. When Toyota advertises, it is not selling a specific vehicle to a specific person, but simply making consumers aware of the name and the product's strong points so they will go to a Toyota showroom where the sales approach is used. Similarly, as you make contact in person, in writing and over the phone, your aim is for them to remember you, your strengths, and your interests. Not until you respond to a call informing you about an opening will you be in a situation where you can "sell" yourself.

Highlight the names of people you know who practice in the area, those you spoke to while informational interviewing, names that kept coming up in your conversations and research, and others that would likely be "warm" contacts or those who may be willing to make a call on your behalf, such as friends, family, and alumni/ae.

Call and attempt to set up a promotional interview, explaining your interest in that area and asking for fifteen to twenty minutes to discuss the field and your search for a position. Make it clear that you assume he or she does not have a position available. Do not, unless asked, send your resume.

If you are successful and do have the opportunity to meet, remember that the objective is to make the interviewer aware of your background, interest, skills, experience, commitment to the area, and availability so that you will be contacted if there is an opening in the future or, more likely, the interviewer will pass on your name and resume to someone else who has an opening in the future. Ask about other people and organizations to contact and which professional groups are active in this area. Leave a copy of your resume and request it be passed along to others.

In a few cases, the interviewer will realize how much he or she needs help only because of the talk with you and make you an immediate offer. In addition to the many full-time positions which are out there, there are many additional employers who could use your help, but are not willing or able to assume the responsibility for another full-time employee. If you are prepared to accept a position working 20–25 hours a week, mention your interest in part-time employment. This may be ideal for graduating students who have family commitments or other part-time employment opportunities and could eventually lead to a full-time position in your field of choice.

Get Involved

The approach you have taken, by following this book's recommendations, is to decide first on the field you want to be in and then get involved. Let's say you have decided that your goal is to provide legal services to reduce the dangers to society arising from damage to our environment. You should begin immersing yourself in the issues and concerns of environmental law, so you can say to yourself, "I *am* an environmental lawyer." Take courses, work or volunteer on a part-time basis, and join a bar association committee or other professional organization of environmental activists.

If your choice is immigration law, join the board of the local chapter of the American Immigration Lawyers Association or take a case for an organization that represents aliens at deportation hearings. If you are interested in families and children, join the family law or mediation committee of a bar association or an alternative dispute resolution organization.

Many make the mistake of not joining a local, state, or national bar association until after they start their first job as a lawyer. To delay until you have a position would be consistent with the passive "placement" mentality. You are in control, act now and get involved with those who work in your area of interest. In addition to the satisfaction you will receive from your volunteer efforts, you will learn a lot and have opportunities to meet those who share your concerns. Many will become aware of you, your competence, your commitment, and refer you for positions you would be suited for.

Selling Yourself

One of your contacts calls you and says that a friend of his needs some help and, based on your contact's comments, would like you to forward your resume to her. What now? Let this next story be instructive.

The Public Interest Law Career Planning Center forwarded to a number of law schools an ad for a work/study position which stated the duties of the position as follows:

> The student would: draft letters and make calls to lawyers, law school career planners, and public interest employees; coordinate projects and organizing efforts; prepare for meetings and conferences; do research for and draft articles; assist in the development of public interest law career planning materials and resources; and perform administrative and clerical chores.

The first person interviewed came to the office without even having taken any time or effort to learn what the Center did. Once it was explained, he acknowledged that it was not at all what he was interested in. Not one of those who responded in writing indicated in their initial cover letter that they knew what the Center did. None highlighted in their resumes the skills needed by a nonprofit organization.

If you respond to an ad, find out ahead of time whether the organization does what interests you. Your cover letter should reflect some knowledge of the place you are sending your resume and further complement it by highlighting experiences which will be valuable to the potential employer. For example, if your interest is in family law, your cover letter can point out that you have experience dealing with agencies, your work with special needs children while an undergrad, and your counseling background.

In three or less sentences, tell why you are right for the position. Perhaps it's your skills, your interest, or your experience. Include information that would not be on your resume, e.g., your career objectives, why you chose this particular area of law and why you are interested in the organization. For example, your letter might include the following wording:

> As my resume indicates, I am interested in working on behalf of senior citizens, and have had a number of internships with organizations which represent them and others underserved by the legal profession. My interest in elder law issues began when I tried to help my parents resolve my grandparent's problems with nursing homes. I

understand that your firm is well known for its work representing elderly clients.

The Interview

Congratulations! You received a call and now have an appointment to talk about the opening. If you were looking for positions not publicly advertised, it is likely that potential employers will not have drawers filled with resumes so the fact that the person doing the hiring has contacted you is another reason for optimism.

In fact, it is possible that you will be the only person under consideration. Your primary competition is yourself. You will know what you want to do with your degree, where, and why. *You will know your strengths. You will believe in yourself and walk in confident that you are the most competent, most qualified person for the position.*

Prepare as if you were going into court or a negotiation session. From your perspective, the interview is an opportunity to first show that you have the skills and experiences required for the position. In addition, it offers a chance to ask questions to determine whether or not the position is consistent with your own personal and professional goals and will use the skills you have or want to develop.

From the employer's perspective, the interview is a time to evaluate your work history, to get a sense of your commitment, your experience, your potential, your ability to communicate, and your personality. It is likely that your work, school, and volunteer experiences listed in your resume or cover letter will form the basis for the discussion. Therefore, by choosing which past experiences to emphasize in order to demonstrate your suitability, you have influenced the direction of the conversation. Know your resume and know why you chose this firm or organization as you head into the interview.

At the close of the interview restate your interest and ask if there is any additional information the employer would like. Later that day, jot down some notes and evaluate the interview. Were your questions answered satisfactorily? Did you forget important questions? Send a thank you note to the interviewer which includes any important relevant information omitted during the interview.

Making a Decision

If you are offered a position, you need to ask yourself "Do I really want it?" Based on questions you asked during the interview, evaluate the extent to which the position is consistent with your own goals, values, and skills. You may again want to complete the "Characteristics and Goals in Your Ideal Workplace" exercise at this time. If there is a clear and strong conflict, have the strength to reject it keeping in mind the high ratio of dissatisfied lawyers and the fact that you are probably saving yourself from starting down the same road.

If you accept a position in your field of choice which uses your skills and matches your priorities, congratulate yourself. You are among the few who have decided to take control over the process. You are on the road to career satisfaction.

10
Reassessment and the Career

A friend told me that a number of years ago, as the new dean of a just-established graduate school of business, he outlined his vision for the school which included no on-campus interviewing. He stated that the system was artificial and deceptive and it gave students the incorrect idea that this was how to find jobs. Perhaps, for some graduates, OCI made the job search easier in the short term, but in the long run, they were done a disservice. They did not learn how to search for opportunities as they would surely have to do several times over the course of their careers. Needless to say, he was overruled and an on-campus interview program was immediately established.

The MacCrate Report provides additional reason for optimism by its comments on p. 236 about the fundamental professional value, the obligation to promote justice, fairness and morality in one's daily practice.

> Law school deans, professors, administrators and staff must not only promote these values by words, but must so conduct themselves as to convey to students that these values are essential ingredients of our profession. Too often, the Socratic method of teaching emphasizes qualities that have little to do with justice, fairness and morality in daily practice. Students too easily gain the impression that wit .... and dazzling performance are more important than the personal moral values that lawyers must possess and that the profession must espouse. The promotion of these values requires no resources and no institutional changes. It does require commitment. (MacCrate Report, p. 236)

Law school graduates, like business school graduates, are likely to have five or more "careers" in their professional life. Lawyers no longer remain in one position from graduation to retirement. The artificial OCI approach leaves them unprepared to make a transition from their first position to the next.

In contrast, the career planning and job search techniques emphasized in this book are something you will use over and over again throughout your professional life. What are your goals and skills? Explore your options. Decide on one direction. Find opportunities. Evaluate them. Accept a position. Evaluate your position. What are your goals and skills? Explore your options. Decide on one direction. Find opportunities. Evaluate them. Accept a position. Evaluate your position.

Your first position may not be perfect, but because you chose it based on what you thought was good for you, it is much more likely that you will derive some benefit from it. The next one will be easier to find because of what you have learned about yourself and the practice of law. Your career path will not necessarily be a clearly defined ascent from the bottom to the top rung in an organization. There are no clear beginnings, middles, or ends. It will be a process, hopefully a series of positive and rewarding experiences.

But through it all, there will be one constant—you are taking control over the decision-making process on all issues relating to your career and your life. What you do and where you end up are to a great extent up to you.

The lack of self-confidence which may begin in law school sometimes continues long after graduation. Many graduates are not optimistic about their prospects. I have found many who, in a discussion about possible openings with nonprofit organizations such as social service organizations, hospitals, or foundations, begin by listing reasons why they would not be qualified.

If your law school experience or a bad employment situation has shaken your confidence, you may need to remind yourself of how much you have already accomplished as a student, employee, or volunteer. Unless you believe in yourself and take time to list all that you have to offer, you will become a victim of the Green Man.

Those who don't believe in themselves limit their options. They often accept a position where they can shine in the reflected glory, telling themselves that working in a place that has "prestige" will "look good" on their resumes. When you represent a client, however, the client cares more about whether or not you know what you are doing. If you ever expect to start your own practice or institution, neither you nor your client will care that you once worked for an important law firm if your experience there did not teach you how to represent someone.

Remind yourself that you have one of the most competent, best trained minds in this country and you are critically needed by millions of underserved members of the public. There are thousands of ways to help them. Know that you never have to take a position where your talents are unappreciated or wasted, or where you are abused or misused.

Conclusion

If you entered law school with the goal of "doing something that matters," choosing a career serving the legal needs of the public will provide you with opportunities to do that. By taking steps now, you can begin mapping out your career and heading off the dissatisfaction that many lawyers face.

Many of your classmates will face the job hunting process with resignation trying desperately to find a job, any job, even if it's one they don't want. They may tell themselves it's just for a few years until school loans are paid off, ignoring the disquieting feeling that in reality it may be for keeps.

In contrast, you will be buoyed by the excitement and enthusiasm that accompanies the quest for a valuable prize. If you believe in yourself and take control of your life, you may very well be the happiest person at your own tenth year reunion.

But keep in mind that career planning takes time and effort. As busy as you are now, you may never again have the luxury of time as you have during the remainder of your last year in law school to accomplish so much of this process. You will possibly regret it if you don't spend at least as much time as you might devote to one law school course.

Think of where you want to be five years from now. Imagine yourself invited by your law school to be on a panel with other attorneys discussing their work. Imagine yourself talking about what you are doing, the excitement, satisfaction, and happiness you derive from your work; how important it is to you to be contributing to the common good and the cause of social justice; your feelings of self-respect and self confidence; how much your efforts are needed; the positive aspects of your workplace and the respect you have for colleagues there; and how compatible your work is with your personal values and professional goals.

Your professional degree provides you with a unique opportunity and a privilege few have—the ability to secure a position in a place where you are comfortable, where you serve those you want to serve, and where you will have control over your career and your life. It is the key to having the flexibility to redefine your career to suit your personal needs and those of your family. Being a professional offers opportunities to continually learn and improve your skills, to develop as a professional, and to grow as an individual as you become more aware of those who need your help. Your professional life holds the possibility of autonomy, satisfaction, integrity, self-respect, and, most meaningful of all, the prospect of sleeping well after a long day on the job and waking up looking forward to going to work.

And all you have to do is take control.

Bibliography

Legal Education

Legal Education and Professional Development—An Educational Continuum, Report of the Task Force on Law Schools and the Profession: Narrowing the Gap, (The MacCrate Report), American Bar Association Section of Legal Education and Admissions to the Bar, 1992.

Stover, R., *Making It and Breaking It,* University of Illinois, 1989.

Bourque, J., *Public Loss,* 1990.

Career Planning

Arron, D., *What Can You Do with a Law Degree?* Niche Press, 1994.

Bolles, R., *What Color is Your Parachute?,* Ten Speed Press, Berkeley, CA, 1994.

Munneke, G.; *The Legal Career Guide: From Law Student to Lawyer,* American Bar Association Law Student Division, 1992.

Munneke, G. and Henslee, W.; *Nonlegal Careers for Lawyers,* American Bar Association Law Student Division, 1994.

Public interest guides published by law schools (i.e., Harvard's *Public Interest Job Search Guide* 1994 and NYU's *Public Service Job Search Resource Booklet* 1994–95.

Byers, M., *Lawyers in Transition,* The Barkley Company, Inc.

Public Interest Advocate, Public Interest Clearinghouse

NAPIL Connection & Close Up

NAPIL Guide to Public Interest Career Resources 1993/1994

The Legal Press

The following publications will be useful in providing names of practitioners and organizations in your chosen field and legal issues.

The ABA Journal, American Bar Association, 750 North Lake Shore Drive, Chicago, IL 60611 (Published monthly.) In addition to *The ABA Journal,* the ABA has over 30 sections and forum committees; i.e., Family Law, Individual Rights & Responsibilities, Natural Resources, Energy & Environmental Law, which each have their own publications and offer student membership. For further information, call the ABA Service Center at (312) 988-5522.

National Law Journal

American Lawyer

Lawyers Weekly USA